CO-AVX-775

BEGINNER
SUNDAY SCHOOL WORK

Beginner
SUNDAY SCHOOL WORK

By

HAZEL N. STRICKLAND

and

MATTIE C. LEATHERWOOD

THE SUNDAY SCHOOL BOARD
OF THE
SOUTHERN BAPTIST CONVENTION
NASHVILLE, TENNESSEE

Printed in the United States of America
2.5AL493

CONTENTS

INTRODUCTION

Mrs. Hazel N. Strickland and Miss Mattie C. Leatherwood have put into the pages of this book the fine art of working for and with Beginners in the Sunday school.

For a number of years Mrs. Strickland has served as Beginner superintendent in the Woodlawn Baptist Church, Birmingham, Alabama. She has been a regular contributor to the publications of the Baptist Sunday School Board. Much of the material in this book is the outgrowth of her effective ministry to four- and five-year-old children.

Miss Leatherwood has devoted her life to Sunday school work. For seventeen years she gave supervision and leadership for Southern Baptists in the interest of little children. At the request of the Sunday School Board she collaborated with Mrs. Strickland in the preparation of the manuscript for this book. She makes grateful acknowledgment to the Department of Church Music for the privilege of adapting and using in Chapter 5 her original material which appeared in the book *Let Us Sing*.

Beginner Sunday School Work is one of two books in the Beginner Specialization Unit in the Sunday School Training Course offered by the Sunday School Board of the Southern Baptist Convention.

J. N. BARNETTE, *Secretary*
THE SUNDAY SCHOOL DEPARTMENT

FOREWORD

The Sunday School Training Course

The Sunday School Training Course prepared by the Sunday School Department of the Baptist Sunday School Board is one of the major means of promoting Sunday school work. Its influence is limited only by its use.

The six sections of the course include studies in Bible, doctrines, evangelism, Sunday school leadership and administration, teaching, age group studies, and special studies. The range of the course is broad, for the field of Sunday school work is broad and requires comprehensive and specific training. Sixteen books are required for the completion of each Diploma.

The study of the Training Course is not to be limited to the present Sunday school workers. Most churches need twice as many workers as are now enlisted. This need can be supplied by training additional workers now. Members of the Young People's and Adult classes and older Intermediates should be led to study these books, for thereby will their service be assured. Parents will find help as they study what the Sunday school is trying to do.

Write to your state Sunday school secretary or to the Sunday School Department, Baptist Sunday School Board, Nashville 3, Tennessee, for a list of the books and other information.

Special Note to Instructors:

During your teaching of this book will you check with the Sunday school superintendent and see if an accurate record of training for the workers is kept. If not, please urge him to set up such a file with an associate superintendent of training in charge. File cards for this purpose will be supplied free of charge upon request. For further information, write to the Sunday School Department, Baptist Sunday School Board, Nashville 3, Tennessee.

J. N. Barnette
Secretary, Sunday School Department
Baptist Sunday School Board

DIRECTIONS FOR THE STUDY OF THIS BOOK

I. FOR TEACHERS OF THE COURSE

1. Ten class periods of forty-five minutes each are needed for the completion of a book.

2. Teachers of classes are given, without special examination, the same award as is provided for the classes which they teach.

II. FOR MEMBERS OF THE TRAINING CLASS

1. The student must be fifteen years of age or older.

2. The student must attend at least six forty-five minute class periods. Where students attended as many as five class periods, an award can be granted only when the following method is used:

Take the usual written examination on the chapters studied and discussed in class.

Study the remaining chapters of the book in accordance with the requirements of the individual method and hand the paper to the class teacher.

3. The student must take a written examination, making a minimum grade of 70 per cent.

4. The student must certify that the textbook has been read. (In rare cases where students may find it impracticable to read the book before the completion of the classwork, the teacher may accept a promise to read the book carefully within the next two weeks.)

III. FOR INDIVIDUAL STUDY

Those who for any reason wish to study the book without the guidance of a teacher will use one of the following methods:

1. Write answers to the questions printed in the book, or

2. Write a development of the chapter outlines.

If the first method is used, the student will study the book and then with the open book write answers to the printed questions.

If the second method is used, the student will study the book and then with the open book write a development of the chapter outlines.

Students may find profit in studying the text together, but individual papers are required. Carbon copies or duplicates in any form cannot be accepted.

All written work done by such students should be sent to the state Sunday school secretary.

CHAPTER OUTLINE

NOTING INDIVIDUAL DIFFERENCES
  Physical Makeup
  Mental Capacity and Development
  Social Ease
  Religious Background

DISCOVERING SOME COMMON CHARACTERISTICS
  Restricted Range of Interests
  Insatiable Curiosity
  Limited Ideas of Time and Space
  Concrete-Mindedness
  Vivid Imagination
  High Suggestibility
  Native Imitation

CONSIDERING SOME OUTSTANDING NEEDS
  Awareness of God's Love and Care
  Training and Experience in Worship
  Experience in Living with Others
  Patterns of Right Conduct

CHAPTER 1

STUDYING BEGINNER CHILDREN

No phase of work for which a Sunday school is responsible is more important, more far-reaching, and more in accord with the expressed wishes of Jesus than a tender ministry to children four and five years of age.

In a properly graded Sunday school these children are Beginners. Many of them have been members of the school since their names were placed on the Cradle Roll soon after they were born. A few of them have had experience in a Nursery Class, but for the most part they are really "beginners" in regular attendance upon the sessions of the school. They are beginners in adventuring away from home and beginners in adjusting to group experiences.

What are these children like? What are their needs and possibilities? Only as the answers to these questions are found can the school intelligently plan and effectively minister to them. An understanding of the children is necessary not only to the wise selection of workers but also to the provision of proper equipment and the choice of materials and methods. Every item of furniture, every piece of lesson material, and every procedure used with them should meet a definite need in their lives.

NOTING INDIVIDUAL DIFFERENCES

No two Beginners are alike. They look different and act differently because they are different in body and mind and in the experiences that have come to them in their four or five years of life.

PHYSICAL MAKEUP

The children are no longer chubby, roly-poly, or round. As their height has increased, their arms and legs have grown longer in proportion to their bodies, resulting in more slenderness. There are noticeable differences in height, however, and some of the children are pale and thin while others are rosy and well proportioned.

These outward differences are evidences of even greater invisible variances. Some children are nervous and easily overstimulated and others tend to be quiet and slow to respond. Some have boundless energy and others are listless. Some have a good deal of endurance; others tire easily. A few have undergone considerable exposure and developed the antibodies which protect them from germs, but most of them have been so shielded and protected that they become easy victims of every disease to which they are exposed.

MENTAL CAPACITY AND DEVELOPMENT

Even wider than the physical differences are the mental differences of the children. They differ both in their inborn capacities and rates of growth and in their development as a result of their surroundings and experiences. Usually a child, whatever his capacity, who lives where things are going on and where his needs are being considered and taken care of, develops faster than one who has a monotonous existence. A child who has varied and rich experiences often attains a higher state of development for his age than an even brighter child who has less stimulus to growth.

For example, one child may be an eager seeker after knowledge because he has had many contacts with interesting things and interesting persons, while another may be dull and uninterested because his early questionings have been hushed and his curiosity dulled. One may love stories, good music, celebrations of the various festival days, and conversation about the things of nature or even things that are going on in the world because he hears and sees and talks about the things at home. Another who is just as old and just as well fed and well clothed may care nothing for such things because no one has taken the trouble to awaken his interest in them. One may appreciate beauty which another never sees. One may love God and want to hear more of him, while another may think of him as a super-policeman.

These differences manifest themselves particularly in such matters as vocabulary, reasoning ability, self-control and self-direction, perseverance, and the length of attention span.

Vocabulary and reasoning ability.—Some children continually amaze their elders by their use of new and lengthy words. "What a pretty airplane!" said an adult visitor to five-year-old Lloyd. "Yes," he answered, "it is an amphibian. See the pontoons?"—thus using two words that were new to the adult.

Other children are handicapped by meager vocabularies. This was true of the child who with shining, appreciative eyes turned from the window and said to a teacher, "Birds yell around the church all the time."

Each child's vocabulary, however large, is limited to his own particular opportunities and experiences. For this reason, one cannot assume that any group of Beginners has a large fund of words common to all.

Ordinarily, Beginners have developed very little reasoning ability, but just as their familiarity with words frequently surprises older people, so do instances of reasoning frequently show unusual ability.

On one occasion a group was discussing the need for sending teachers to other lands to tell about Jesus.

"We ought not to send any to Japan," suggested John. "My daddy says they are mean and fight too much."

"Well, that's why we should send them teachers," countered Dan, thus proving that some Beginners think deeply.

Self-control and self-direction.—There are marked differences in self-control and self-direction among normal Beginner children, due in part to physical and mental makeup and in part to training. A healthy, normal four-year-old who has had intelligent teaching may be expected to have some control of crying, to wait with reasonable patience for things he wants, to control bodily functions, and to use some of the simpler courtesy forms. To a reasonable extent he will be obedient, tidy, kindly, and courageous. The five-year-old will have grown noticeably in each of these controls.

If, however, a child is accustomed to being treated as if he were a baby, he will cry, be untidy or even unclean, and have no idea of obeying. He may even have temper tantrums when he is thwarted or develop the habit of doing the opposite to what is suggested or commanded.

As in self-control, so in self-direction Beginners differ greatly, but the most deficient need not have everything done for them. Even the four-year-olds usually can do much more than some adults are inclined to permit, though this ability must often be developed at Sunday school, especially in the case of children who have been pampered at home. All normal Beginners can be trained to care for their own coats and hats, put away toys, help take care of equipment, and to remember the behavior suitable in Sunday school.

Perseverance.—Another point at which there is great difference is in the matter of perseverance. An inability to stay with any given task or interest may be due to physical or mental limitations but more often it is the result of a child's not being trained or even being permitted to complete what he begins. A child who has too many toys or too many activities from which to choose is handicapped in this respect. So is one whose elders think of his activities as unimportant and who interrupt him at their convenience, thereby discouraging rather than encouraging him to finish what he has begun.

A child who is given a few minutes' warning before he is called from his work or play, and thus encouraged to complete the blockhouse he may be building or the picture he may be making, is greatly helped in the matter of perseverance.

Attention span.—While the attention span of all Beginners is short, there are marked differences within this limit. As a rule, where four- and five-year-olds are grouped together, the longer attention span of the older children is noticeable. Differences because of home experiences are noticeable here also. Children accustomed to listening to Bible passages and to stories are usually more interested and can give attention longer than those who lack this background of training. Beginners who play regularly with older children can give attention longer than those whose companions are adults or children of their own age.

Children of this age are more apt to concentrate on doing things than on listening or talking. While a story may bore them if it is longer than three or four minutes, they will be interested in a self-chosen activity for eight or ten more minutes and in a game much longer. One Beginner group wrapped packages and packed them for a family at Christmas for a period of thirty minutes after hearing a two-minute story and engaging in a one-minute conversation about the need.

SOCIAL EASE

Perhaps there are greater variances in the ability of children to get along with others than in either physical or mental capacity or individual development. In any group of Beginners many different social attitudes can be observed. Frequently there is a "bossy" child who likes to issue orders, to scold, or to protect. He is usually, but not always, an older child and he often comes from a home where his ego is repressed.

Occasionally there is a child with a show-off attitude, springing from a desire to attract attention which he expresses in ways varying from rolling on the floor to taking the greatest care in cutting and pasting. Often there are less self-reliant children who follow the "show off" by imitation. Last of all, there are the children who show that highest of social attitudes, co-operation. They are most likely to be children who have a happy home environment where grownups and children work and share and have good times together.

RELIGIOUS BACKGROUND

Every group represents a variety of religious backgrounds. Much as one could wish it, a joyous Christian home is not the heritage of every Beginner. In many homes one parent is not a Christian or is an indifferent one. In some homes the parents are thoughtless about religious matters and in others they are too impatient and lacking in understanding for the most wholesome development of the children.

In an occasional home there may seem to be no regard for religion at all, but it may be assumed that any parents who send a child to Sunday school have some desire for the help that the Sunday school can give. Any child, regardless of his home environment and what he knows or does not know, can be interested in God and the things of God.

DISCOVERING SOME COMMON CHARACTERISTICS

Fortunately the ways in which the children are alike are as numerous as the ways in which they are different. Their common characteristics and interests provide a starting point for the special ministry which a church undertakes and also give confidence in the making of plans. It is well to consider some of these characteristics.

RESTRICTED RANGE OF INTERESTS

Instead of thinking of themselves only, even four-year-olds are beginning to adjust themselves to the wishes and needs of others. Five-year-olds are readily moving out into the world of playmates at home and classmates at Sunday school. Nevertheless, the range of Beginner interests is still limited. The home, the Sunday school, the familiar natural surroundings, and a few outside places which hold some special appeal, are the boundaries of the children's world. Even when they go outside these restricted areas, the things they "see" are the familiar interests of their everyday lives.

INSATIABLE CURIOSITY

Beginners never tire of asking questions. In this way they express a readiness to learn and also furnish a key to what they can learn. They rarely ask foolish questions and often seek information about the most profound subjects. Because they really want to know, they frequently ask, "Who made God?" "What does God look like?" "Where is heaven?" and other similar questions which are difficult to answer. In all fairness, however, they must be answered to the children's satisfaction.

The children's interest in natural phenomena often leads to questions about God's creations that are invaluable in helping them to understand the nature of God. Even as little fingers ask unspoken questions and are answered by the shape and smoothness of an apple or the prickliness of a chestnut burr, little lips ask questions of wonder and the children learn from wise answers that God is all wise and good.

LIMITED IDEAS OF TIME AND SPACE

It is generally accepted that at this age children do not comprehend in any appreciable degree the extent of time and space. "I had my birthday last week," said a child when his birthday had been several months past, but this did not mean that he was telling an untruth. "Last week" to Beginners may mean any past time even as "tomorrow" may mean any time in the future. Thus, "Once in the land where Jesus lived" is more satisfying to them than "Two thousand years ago in Palestine."

CONCRETE-MINDEDNESS

Symbolic expressions so meaningful to older people have no significance for Beginners because they are concrete minded. "Crosses," "crowns," and "clean hearts" have only the literal meanings for them. A "lost lamb" is not a lost soul but a real lost baby sheep and a "light" is a flashlight or a lamp.

Beginners are also confused by abstract statements. The verse "God is love" can have no meaning for them if they are not helped to feel his love through song and story. They find difficulty also with such abstract words as "helpfulness" and "obedience" but are quick to respond to suggestions for helping Mother and "obeying" or "minding Mother."

VIVID IMAGINATION

The children's vivid imagination is one of God's choicest gifts to them and is a great asset to learning. Through imagination they can enter into those experiences of others which have some elements in common to their own. This saves them much of the slow trial-and-error learning which otherwise could come to them only through their own experiences. The greatest value of the story is that the children enter into it through the gate of imagination. Without imagination they could never realize God's presence and care nor the friendship of Jesus. It is a gift to be appreciated and cultivated. It should never be blunted, misunderstood, or abused.

HIGH SUGGESTIBILITY

Imagination is responsible for high suggestibility, another valuable asset to learning. The simple suggestion, "It would be nice to have some lumberman haul off the blocks," may clear the floor like magic. "If Mary had some crayons, she could make a nice picture too," may be cheerfully suggested and result in a sharing experience for a child whose interest is self-centered.

If a teacher will speak in a soft low voice when the children are inclined to be noisy, they will lower their voices more quickly than if she raises hers to suggest it. They also respond quickly to suggestions for desirable behavior which pictures and stories offer. It should be remembered, however, that they as readily accept and act upon suggestions for undesirable actions. It is important then that they be given opportunities to practice carrying out suggestions for desirable conduct, for in this way they will learn to think and to choose the right.

NATIVE IMITATION

It is as natural for the children to imitate the activities they see going on about them as it is for them to ask questions. They imitate the movement, the tone of voice, and the conduct of adults and other children, and much of their imitation is unconscious. Far more important than their imitation of another's actions and mannerisms is their absorption of the likes and dislikes and attitudes of others. Children may grow strong through imitating a grownup's quiet poise and confidence in herself to meet whatever situation arises, or they may imitate a nervous, flighty person's attitude with disastrous results.

CONSIDERING SOME OUTSTANDING NEEDS

Even a brief study of Beginner children cannot be brought to a close without some consideration of their needs which Sunday school teachers can hope to meet.

AWARENESS OF GOD'S LOVE AND CARE

From the third through the fifth year the children's ideas of God are definitely developing. What these ideas shall be depends upon the atmosphere of the homes and the guidance or lack of guidance given by parents and teachers.

During this period the children need to discover God in the world about them—in nature and in people. They need to learn that everything which makes them happy is a gift from God, and that they can feel secure in his love and care. They need to find in Jesus, the best Friend of little children, one who knows how God feels and how he wants children to feel and act. They need to understand something of how God works in his world and how he uses people to help him. They need to learn also that they please God when they help other people.

When parents are careless and unmindful of their obligation, the church has an increased responsibility for giving the children this Christian concept of God.

TRAINING AND EXPERIENCE IN WORSHIP

As the children become more aware of God's love and care, they need training and experience in reaching out to him in prayer, praise, and giving. They need to know that they can talk to God any time and anywhere, that he is interested in all that they do, and is always ready to help them. It is important also for them to learn during these early years that God sometimes says no to their requests because what they ask is not good for them.

EXPERIENCE IN LIVING WITH OTHERS

Because they are still near the self-centered period of babyhood, Beginners need definite help in adjusting favorably to the various groups of which they find themselves members.

As they work and play together in Sunday school, they become aware of the property rights of others. They learn to take turns, to play fair, and to be co-operative and helpful. Through satisfying experiences they learn that helping and sharing are as interesting as being helped and getting, and that such practices make for happy living with others.

Eagerness to help children get along with others and the desire to discourage "showing off" sometimes lead to the mistake of ignoring the need of every child to stand out worthily from the group and to be recognized as a self-respecting individual. Each child should be given legitimate opportunities for creative effort, for exercising leadership, and for using his special gifts to help him gain that feeling of individual success and personal merit which is necessary to a well-rounded personality.

A child's acceptance by his group and the satisfying of his ego are necessary to his happy social adjustment, and their importance cannot be overemphasized. Any child can better fit himself into the group if he is sure that he is loved and wanted for his own sake. Both the too-timid child who stands back from the group and the too-obstreperous child who demands more than his share of attention are usually uncertain about how they stand.

The timid child needs a word of praise when he does anything satisfactorily even though it be only a carefully pasted picture or a neatly folded note to take to Mother. The overbearing child may be timid, too, and hungry for love and approval rather than for favors. When a child is sure of himself, he tends to take his normal place in the group and abide by its known rules.

Children from large families, who have many neighborhood playmates, and from homes where there is only one child and no playmates, need experiences they find at Sunday school. Members of this group are about the same age, have similar capacities, interests, and physical development. They make about the same mistakes and need to learn much the same things. In this group there are no older brothers to tease them or older sisters to pamper them. Children who happen to be the oldest in their own homes and who may override younger sisters or brothers learn at Sunday school that such conduct is not approved. They must take their places among their peers and take care of themselves.

PATTERNS OF RIGHT CONDUCT

In learning to adjust to others, Beginners need patterns of conduct which will make them approved members of the group. Some of these patterns are such simple "rules" of Sunday school as: "We carry our chairs with the legs down." "When one child has finished speaking, another may speak" and "We all keep quiet and listen when Miss Mary plays about Christmas." These typify rules which in practice set up conduct patterns for safety and courtesy in Sunday school. Through particular experiences of obeying, taking turns, sharing, facing consequences, helping, being kind, and when necessary of feeling and saying, "I'm so sorry," conduct patterns may be set up as they are needed, no matter what the "lesson" for the day may be.

The patterns of conduct approved at Sunday school will not automatically carry over into the home or other groups. There must be some teaching to bridge the gap and wholehearted co-operation between parents and teachers if patterns are to be worked in the best of all laboratories—the home. As an illustration, at Sunday school a child may get, through story or through play, patterns of sharing at home or of helping Mother. However, if Mother gives him no opportunity to share and does not have time for him to help, he does not make sharing or helpfulness a part of his home experience and through much practice make it a part of his character.

Parents and teachers, then, must join hands in meeting these outstanding needs of Beginner children. They must work together so that the children may better learn of God's love and care. They must see to it that the children have training and experiences in worship. In the homes parents must create an atmosphere in which the children can take their rightful places in happy family groups and among their playmates and neighbors. In the Sunday school teachers must help the children learn to live and work together happily with others outside their normal home groups. Both must supply many conduct patterns to give the children daily experience in choosing that which is right for one of their years. By such co-operation, between the home and the Sunday school each child can be given the religious teaching and training he needs at this stage of his development.

CHAPTER OUTLINE

CHAPTER II

ENLISTING BEGINNER WORKERS

The story is told of two children in the Holy Land who went one afternoon into the hills to play. As darkness began to fall, their anxious mother started out to look for them. She had walked only a short way when she saw them running to meet her. Into her arms she gathered them as words of explanation came tumbling from their lips. "We have been out with ———," they said. "You need not tell me," she answered quickly. "I know you have been with Simon, the spice seller, gathering spices."

Even as the heavy fragrance of his spices clings to those who tarry long with the spice seller, so does the gentle fragrance of the Master's spirit breathe in the personality of Beginner workers who have been "with Jesus."

SELECTING WITH CARE

Although the workers in a Beginner department hold different positions and have different responsibilities and duties, they are all "teachers" to the children. Where they lead, the children follow with utmost confidence. The "teachers" make the department. For this reason, the words "teacher" and "teachers" are used in later chapters when reference is made to any or all of the workers.

The pastor and the general superintendent should select the teacher, who also acts as superintendent; then she should work with them in discovering and enlisting her co-workers.

Young mothers who are having daily contacts with small children make excellent teachers. So do older mothers with wider experience and increased wisdom who have kept their understanding of the world where children live and are not tied down with home cares. Kindergarten and Nursery school teachers bring to the work rich experience and specialized training. Business women with mother hearts and a willingness to make necessary preparation also become efficient and trustworthy teachers.

Young girls of Intermediate age are not qualified for Beginner work because they lack the rich understanding which life experiences bring. On the other hand, some women who are well qualified by experience are not young enough in years or spirit to meet the demands which working with these active children makes on physical strength and nerves.

NECESSARY QUALIFICATIONS

Little children absorb many of the ideals and attitudes, as well as the manners, of the grownups with whom they associate. For this reason, those who are responsible for selecting and enlisting the teachers should carefully consider their personality and qualifications.

Definite Christian experience.—One morning a man, who boasted of his unbelief, greeted a child with the question, "Where are you going so early?"

"I'm going to Sunday school," she answered.

"Why do you go to Sunday school?"

"To learn about God."

"What makes you think there is a God?" continued the man.

"My teacher knows him," replied the child without a moment's hesitation.

Every Beginner teacher should *know God*. She should know him as Jesus portrayed him, as the Bible reveals him, as the lives of Christian men and women interpret him, and as the wonders of nature show forth his power. She should know him because of her own personal experience of grace through faith in Jesus as her Saviour and Lord.

She should not only be a Christian but also a growing Christian—growing in grace and knowledge, growing in her prayer life and in her understanding of God's Word, growing most of all in her likeness to Jesus. Her trusting, cheerful Christian life should make it easy for the children to catch her spirit and learn to know God and to feel that Jesus is their loving Friend.

She should be a member of the church in which she teaches and should enter enthusiastically into its plans and programs. Only one who belongs to the church in which she serves can in fairness ask the parents of the children to join it.

Personality attractive to children.—One may be a sincere, growing Christian and yet be unsuited for work with Beginners. Outstanding qualifications which combine to make a personality attractive to Beginners are love, sympathetic understanding, and a happy childlike spirit.

Love for the children.—The suggestion has been made that when Jesus set a child in the midst, he did not choose an adolescent or an infant, but a child four or five years of age. Be that as it may, Beginner children are at such an attractive, winsome age that sometimes a grownup is misled. She may think that she loves children when in reality she only likes their dimpled sweetness, their happy smiles, or their dainty clothes. A real teacher loves more than these outside things. She loves the children themselves, seeing something of their possibilities, and accepting the challenge of their shortcomings and weaknesses. Only so will she do the study and patiently seek the understanding necessary to help them become the children God would have them be.

Sympathetic understanding.—A Beginner teacher should be a real companion of the children in the department. Genuine sympathy implies an understanding between two people so that whatever affects the one similarly affects the other. The problems and joys of little children are very real to them even when they may be amusing to older people. A sympathetic teacher often laughs *with* the children but never *at* them because she understands their viewpoint and accords them the respect she would older persons.

This sympathetic attitude draws the children to the teacher and invites them to share with her experiences that make them happy and to confide in her when something troubles them. It was to a sympathetic, understanding teacher that a little four-year-old said: "My mother loves the baby too much." Quick to see her problem, the teacher helped her to understand the helplessness of babies and the care mothers have to give them. She suggested some things that the child herself could do to help care for the baby. Then that very day she went to see the child's mother. It had not occurred to the mother that her little girl was finding it difficult to make adjustments to the baby being showered with the attentions she formerly received. Thus the teacher helped with a problem that might have had serious consequences on the child's personality.

Happy, childlike spirit.—Unless the children are suppressed to a marked degree, they are naturally happy. They should have a happy teacher. She should share their feeling that every day brings something to be glad about and should wonder with them in a genuine way over God's power and goodness in making a world so beautiful. She should be so childlike in spirit and feel so much at home in the children's world that they will often forget the difference between her age and theirs.

Controlled emotional life.—A Beginner teacher should be willing to make haste slowly in guiding the children. She should be unhurried, calm, and patient, because she knows their limitations. She should be confident and poised because she is prepared. Preparation and experience should help her to be resourceful and to meet with promptness any situation that arises.

Children catch the teacher's spirit of calm assurance and feel secure. They rarely reject the decisions of such a teacher. They move smoothly through the activities of the session. If, however, the teacher is unprepared, unsure, and nervous, the children catch her spirit too. This leads to noisy confusion and behavior problems.

Dependability and co-operation.—Dependability and willingness and ability to work with others are essential. The dependable teacher attends Sunday school every Sunday as a matter of course. She comes on time, which means ahead of time.

Dependability insures regular attendance also at the officers and teachers' meeting. It insures the giving of the proper time and thought to program assignment, whether for the Sunday morning session or the officers and teachers' meeting. Last-minute efforts do not usually produce interesting results. Dependability shows itself in small things like preparing party invitations for a group or keeping faith with a child.

Along with dependability should go a spirit of co-operation or willingness to work with others in the department and in the entire school. Every teacher should gladly do her best to help carry out the plans and purposes of both.

DESIRABLE ATTRIBUTES

In addition to the necessary qualifications which have been given, there are others less important, perhaps, but still greatly to be desired. Other things being equal, true culture, open-mindedness, and a vivid imagination are real assets in dealing with Beginners.

True culture.—A teacher reflects culture in her gracious manner and in her pleasing voice. She proves it by her friendliness and courtesy. She never makes the mistake of speaking to the children in that oversweet voice which has been labeled the "kindergarten voice," but which good kindergarten teachers never use. She has no affectation and always speaks in quiet, sincere tones. She shows the children the same courtesy that she expects of them. It never occurs to her to take a child's toy or work materials without permission or to interrupt when a child is speaking.

It has sometimes been assumed that one does not need to "know much" to teach young children. On the contrary, one can never know enough to answer all their questions or teach them all they need to learn. The best educated person available is none too well informed to teach Beginners.

Open-mindedness.—A mind closed to new ideas is fatal to good teaching. A person who feels in a certain way about things because she has always felt that way and does things in a certain way because she has always done them that way cannot be a truly good teacher. Principles do not change, but methods do and so do ways of living. The teacher must study and think and experiment and be willing to profit by her own mistakes as well as those of others. She must never feel that she "knows children" but find in each new group a fresh challenge to discover the very best methods for teaching and training them.

Vivid imagination.—"You are too tall, you see, to hear the grass grow or to see the way-down roots of things," said a child to her teacher. It was her way of saying, "You have no power of imagination. You can't go with me into the world of make-believe."

Children are quick to sense a teacher's ability to enter wholeheartedly into their flights of fancy and to co-operate in their play experiences. It was really a compliment to their teacher when a group engaged in playing "home" asked her to be the dog. She proved that the compliment was not misplaced when she cheerfully accepted the assignment. Her imagination adds color and vividness to the stories she tells, to the conversation she leads, to the songs she sings. It also helps her to appreciate the experiences that the children themselves relate.

CHALLENGING TO A REAL TASK

The type of teacher needed in a Beginner department will not be interested in a too-easy task. The person of ability wants to do things that call for effort and give promise of results that justify it.

MAGNIFY THE WORK

The importance and far-reaching influence of this ministry to children four and five years of age cannot be overemphasized. The foundations of character and the bent, or trend, of the life's actions and attitudes are established by the time a child is five years old. All his life he will tend to react as he is trained to react during these early years. His whole life will be influenced throughout the years by the attitudes and appreciations he develops now.

PRESENT OPPORTUNITIES AND RESPONSIBILITIES

It is estimated that one of every three children of Beginner age who should be enrolled in Southern Baptist

Sunday schools has not been reached. One of every three is passing through the Beginner years without the Bible teaching and the training in right living which the schools have to offer. All too often this means he is passing through these years without any religious training at all. It is a part of Beginner work to find and enlist these neglected ones.

It is a teacher's responsibility not only to guide and train the children at Sunday school but also to minister to them and their parents in their homes. Often she has opportunity to serve them in times of illness and sorrow. Frequently it is her privilege to share their delights on joyous occasions. Sometimes she is able to help their unsaved parents to become Christians or to contribute to the growth and development of those who are already Christians. These and other opportunities should challenge her to dedicate herself to her work in a spirit of deep consecration.

ORGANIZING FOR EFFECTIVE SERVICE

The number of workers needed depends upon the number of four- and five-year-old children who are enrolled or who are possibilities for enrolment. The presence of too many grownups in a group tends to make the children self-conscious and unnatural in their behavior. Consequently, only the number actually needed to carry on the work efficiently should be enlisted.

The following table will help determine the number of workers that are needed:

Ten or less children—one worker. (This worker will be responsible for all that should be done for the children.) Her duties are as follows:

1. Work in co-operation with the Sunday school superintendent.

2. Study each child in the Beginner group. Know each child's needs, interest, abilities, and experiences. Learn about the child in general, through observation and study.

3. Prepare and make definite teaching plans for Sunday morning.

4. Guide the child in learning experience. (The child is not in Sunday school to play. He is there to learn about God, Jesus, the Bible, the church, and how to live with others.)

5. Visit absentees, new members, and prospects.

6. Mark the children on "Attendance" and "On Time." (Workers are marked on all six points of the Six Point Record System.)

7. Promote home co-operation.

8. Train for more effective service.

9. Participate in workers' meetings promoted by the Sunday school.

Ten to fifteen children—two workers. One worker may be known as superintendent and the other as associate. Their duties may be divided as follows:

SUPERINTENDENT

1. Work in co-operation with Sunday school superintendent.

2. Study each child in the Beginner group. Know each child's needs, abilities, interest, and experiences.

3. Make thorough preparation and definite teaching plans for Sunday morning.

4. Work with associate in guiding each child in learning experiences on Sunday morning.

5. Promote home co-operation.

6. Share with associate visitation responsibilities.

7. Lead out in training efforts.

8. Participate in workers' meetings promoted by Sunday school.

ASSOCIATE

1. Work in co-operation with superintendent.

2. Study each child in the Beginner group. Know each child's needs, abilities, interest, and experiences.

3. Make thorough preparation and definite teaching plans for Sunday morning.

4. Share with superintendent teaching responsibilities on Sunday morning.

5. Visit absentees, new members, and prospects.

6. Mark children on "Attendance" and "On Time." Mark workers on all six points.

7. Serve as pianist.

8. Participate in workers' meetings promoted by Sunday school.

Sixteen to twenty-four children—three workers. (Of the three workers, one may be superintendent and the other two her associates.) Duties may be divided as follows:

SUPERINTENDENT

1. Work in co-operation with Sunday school superintendent.

2. Study each child in the Beginner group. Know each child's needs, abilities, interest, and experiences.

3. Make thorough preparation and definite teaching plans for Sunday morning.

4. Give general directions to all activities on Sunday morning.

5. Promote home co-operation.

6. Plan for and conduct conferences at weekly officers and teachers' meetings or monthly workers' conference.

7. Lead workers in training.

8. Maintain complete organization.

9. Share visitation responsibilities with associate.

Associate

1. Work in co-operation with superintendent.

2. Study each child in the Beginner group. Know each child's needs, abilities, interest, and experiences.

3. Make thorough preparation and definite teaching plans for Sunday morning.

4. Share with other workers teaching responsibilities on Sunday morning.

5. Visit absentees, new members, and prospects of own specific group.

6. Keep records of entire Beginner group.

7. Attend and take part in weekly officers and teachers' meeting or monthly workers' conference.

8. Co-operate in training efforts.

Associate

1. Work in co-operation with superintendent.

2. Study each child in the Beginner group. Know each child's needs, abilities, interest and experiences.

3. Make thorough preparation and definite teaching plans for Sunday morning.

4. Share with other workers teaching responsibilities on Sunday morning.

5. Visit absentees, new members, and prospects of own specific group.

6. Serve as pianist.

7. Attend and take part in weekly officers and teachers' meeting or monthly workers' conference.

8. Co-operate in training efforts.

Twenty-five to fifty children—complete organization. (This organization includes a superintendent, an associate superintendent, a secretary, a pianist, and a teacher or group leader for each ten children.)

SUPERINTENDENT

1. Select and enlist workers in co-operation with the pastor and general superintendent.

2. Maintain a complete organization.

3. Plan the work of the department in accord with general plans for the school.

4. Keep the department graded.

5. Study each child in the Beginner group. Know each child's needs, interest, abilities and experiences.

6. Make thorough preparation and definite teaching plans for Sunday morning.

7. Give general directions to all activities on Sunday morning.

8. Plan for and conduct department conferences at weekly officers and teachers' meeting or monthly workers' conference.

9. Lead workers in program of training and development.

10. Promote home co-operation.

ASSOCIATE SUPERINTENDENT

1. Act as hostess for the department greeting children and visitors at the door.

2. Direct program for enlisting new pupils.

3. Protect the department from interruptions.

4. Attend to administrative details, such as announcements about special meetings, contributions, and pledges.

5. Study carefully the lesson for Sunday morning.

6. Study the children.

7. Attend and take care in the weekly officers and teachers' meeting or monthly conference.

PIANIST

1. Study the children (needs, interests, abilities, and experiences.)

2. Learn how to play for Beginners.

3. Study carefully the lesson for Sunday morning.

4. Work closely with the superintendent in plans for Sunday.

5. Select songs suited to Beginners.

6. Memorize words and music of songs used.

7. Co-operate in the weekly officers and teachers' meeting or monthly conference.

SECRETARY

1. Keep department records.

2. Keep accurate enrolment of department.

3. Classify new pupils.

4. Mark pupils on Sunday morning.

5. Prepare department reports for general secretary.

6. Study carefully the lesson for Sunday morning.

7. Co-operate in the weekly officers and teachers' meeting or monthly conference.

TEACHERS OR GROUP LEADER

1. Study each child in her group, keeping individual record of interests, needs, experiences, and abilities.

2. Make detailed preparation for Sunday morning.

3. Co-operate with the superintendent in plans for Sunday.

4. Plan with superintendent for small group period.

5. Guide the children in learning experiences in centers of interest.

6. Help superintendent in large group period.

7. Attend and take part in the weekly officers and teachers' meeting or monthly workers' conference.

8. Prepare herself mentally and spiritually for her task by studying the Bible systematically, by setting aside a period for personal devotion, and by reading books related to Beginner work.

Teachers or group leaders make their finest contributions to the Sunday morning session as occasions demand and without suggestion except from their own understanding hearts. They are quick to discover children who are self-conscious and unhappy and help them by slipping balls or dolls into their little arms. They offer suggestions about building a wall or a barn when the children are inclined to kick the blocks about. They provide paper doll families just when they are needed for the block homes or churches. They join groups to tell stories or sing appropriate songs when the children are examining pictures.

They suggest ways for keeping the story papers nice and smooth "so mothers can read them" and make sure that party invitations or announcements will get to the homes safely by pinning them to little coats or dresses. They help open unruly purses and untie knots in handkerchiefs where love gifts safely repose. They help to keep up with handkerchiefs, purses, and other personal belongings and listen with interest to all the children want to tell about happenings in their homes, remembering always to guard their confidences as sacred. Indeed, they are grown-up friends who love and are loved and make Sunday school a happy place where children like to gather.

It cannot be emphasized too strongly that conducting a Beginner department is a co-operative enterprise. It is not the superintendent-teacher's department. It is not even the school's. It is God's and all those who work in it faithfully and well are servants of his.

CHAPTER OUTLINE

PLANNING A DEPARTMENT ROOM

    Select the Location
    Allow Ample Floor Space
    Locate Door and Windows
    Consider Walls, Ceiling, and Woodwork
    Arrange Necessary Conveniences

FURNISHING A DEPARTMENT ROOM

    Assure Comfort for the Children
    Provide for Department Activities
    Contribute to Homelike Atmosphere

ADJUSTING SMALL SCHOOL EQUIPMENT

    Use an Available Room
    Screen a Corner
    Improvise Furniture

SELECTING TEACHING MATERIALS

    Southern Baptist Literature
    Record Materials
    Handwork Materials
    Books and Pictures
    Play Equipment

CHAPTER III

PROVIDING EQUIPMENT AND TEACHING
MATERIALS

When a church builds and furnishes a room for Beginner children, it builds and furnishes not for the two short years each of them will spend in the department, but for all the years that follow. An attractive place suitable for happy learning and worship experiences fosters in the children a love and a respect for God's house and for all that goes on there. This attitude when implanted early often abides through life.

PLANNING A DEPARTMENT ROOM

Local conditions vary, and all teachers do not have opportunity to plan their rooms from the beginning as they would like to do but all teachers should know what a department needs and why. They should do all they can to secure the needed equipment under their present circumstances and be ready to offer helpful suggestions to a building committee if an opportunity arises.

Often churches engage in new building projects or find it necessary to enlarge their buildings to provide for growing needs. In such cases, architects and committees responsible for making plans are usually glad to know what teachers of children consider best for their departments and as far as possible to give consideration to their suggestions.

Even in places where the department room is inadequate in size or arrangement, and the church does not plan to make drastic changes in the immediate future, teachers need not become discouraged. They may find in their situation a challenge to make the best possible use of what they have today and continue to work toward the ideal conditions they desire.

They may well remember, too, that there are times when workers do not receive because they do not ask. For example, for more than a year the activities in an adjoining department of a school distracted the attention of the children and interrupted the procedure in a certain Beginner department. Finally, the workers brought the matter to the attention of the general superintendent, who quickly, easily, and inexpensively corrected it by having sound-proof material placed over the double doors between the rooms. Often a difficult situation may be corrected by workers who have imagination and initiative.

SELECT THE LOCATION

The first floor (which means *above* the ground) offers the best location for the department room. The next choice is the second floor. Stairs present a difficulty but not as great as that of a cheerless basement room.

The room should be separated from all others by solid walls. Movable partitions which do not shut out sounds work a hardship on the children who must "keep quiet" to avoid disturbing others and whose attentions are continually distracted by noises of activities on the other side of the partition.

The room should be well lighted and easily accessible from the main corridor. It should never have to be entered by passing through another class or department room.

ALLOW AMPLE FLOOR SPACE

The size of the room should allow the children to move about freely and to engage in various types of activity.

It should not be large enough, however, to preclude a homelike atmosphere. The Department of Church Architecture, Baptist Sunday School Board, gives preference to an oblong room and suggests fourteen square feet of floor space for each person.

"I have fifty children in my department. To provide that much space would make a barnlike room," someone objects. This may be true, but a church should not plan a room for fifty children. When there are more than twenty-five children enrolled, it should begin planning for two departments. More and more, teachers are finding that the informal procedure best suited to the teaching of Beginners can only be carried on in relatively small groups. When the enrolment reaches fifty, a church should make every effort to provide two rooms, each containing at least 350 square feet of floor space.

LOCATE DOOR AND WINDOWS

The singular of the word "door" is used advisedly. One door for entrance and exit is sufficient. It should open outwardly and should be in the rear of the room to protect the department activities against interruptions by late children, visitors, or friends who just peep in through curiosity.

Unless there is a central ventilating system in the church, windows which may be kept open in warm weather and opened often in cold weather are necessary to the children's health and comfort. They should be located along the sides of the room, never at the front where the light will fall in the children's eyes. To furnish proper light and ventilation, window space should measure approximately one-sixth to one-fourth of the floor space.

In addition to furnishing light and ventilation, windows, except in closely built areas, provide view. This is a teaching asset in Beginner work. Clear glass windows that are low and wide permit the children to see God's out-of-doors—the flowers, trees, grass, rain, and snow. Seeing leads to questions, and questions rightly answered lead to knowledge. Again, seeing leads to wonder, and wonder is closely akin to worship.

CONSIDER WALLS, CEILING, AND WOODWORK

Walls not only shut out sights and sounds but also contribute to a sense of security. They lend themselves admirably for use as a background for pictures and other decorations. Semigloss paint which does not reflect light makes one of the most satisfactory finishes. It is sanitary and easily cleaned.

A nine- or ten-foot ceiling is preferable for the room. It should be painted a lighter shade than the walls.

Naturally the height of the ceiling conforms to that of other rooms on the same floor. When this is higher than is desirable for a Beginner department room, the ceiling may be dropped. If this cannot be done, the ceiling color can be brought down the side walls to a height of about nine feet above the floor. This gives the effect of a lower ceiling.

The picture rail extends across the front of the room and follows the pattern of plate rails often used in dining rooms. It may be six or eight inches wide. Besides being grooved it may have a strip tacked along the front edge extending a quarter of an inch above the rail. Placed twenty-seven inches from the floor, this rail makes a satisfactory arrangement for displaying temporary pictures. It is favored over a dado of cork or wallboard because it eliminates the need for thumbtacks, which the children have difficulty in handling and which grownups find very evasive.

Hardwood or well-finished pine should be used for the floor. Concrete is tiring to leg and back muscles. It is also cold and cheerless, and it makes heating the room difficult. Comfort demands a covering of wood or inlaid linoleum. If linoleum is used, it is best to choose the plain or a soft marbelized design. Distinct patterns should be avoided.

Preference is no longer given to blue and white in decorating a Beginner room. The use of richer colors achieves effects with more character and more appeal for the children. Blue-green, gray-green, soft glowing yellows, amber, and the warmer rose tints are among the favored colors, while white enameled woodwork often gives place to natural finished woods.

In choosing the color scheme for a room, teachers will do well to seek expert advice. If this is not available, they may well study colored pictures of successfully treated rooms which appear in magazines, to learn the accepted principles of decoration and the color combinations which insure pleasing results. The following suggestions offer examples of effective color combinations:

For a sunny room—gray-green carpet or linoleum, blue-green or ivory walls, off-white ceiling, ivory or gray woodwork, deep ivory furniture, cretonne draperies with blue-green and gray-green motifs.

For a room needing a warmer treatment—wine color floor covering, soft yellow walls, off-white ceiling, light oak furniture, sheer curtains of an amber tone, cretonne draperies with dark red predominating.

ARRANGE NECESSARY CONVENIENCES

A small coatroom adjoining the department room should be provided for proper care of coats, hats, and other outdoor clothing. Hooks placed low enough for the children to hang up their own things encourage independence. A shelf built above the hooks makes a satisfactory arrangement for hats. Several hooks five or six feet high provide convenience for the teachers. For the sake of their own comfort and to set examples for the children, the teachers should remove their hats and wraps during the Sunday school hour.

A low sanitary fountain, preferably outside the department room, should make drinking water easily available. Toilet facilities suited to the needs of four- and five-year-olds are required also, and a room properly equipped may open from the coatroom or corridor.

FURNISHING A DEPARTMENT ROOM

The furnishings for a department room should be simple, durable, and attractive. They should assure comfort for the children, provide for department activities, and contribute to a pleasing, homelike atmosphere. They need not be expensive. There is a happy medium between a room that is not "pretty" to the children and one whose perfect appointments make them room-conscious and ill at ease.

Assure Comfort for the Children

Physical comfort is necessary to happiness and co-operation. Nothing contributes more to it than proper seating facilities.

Chairs.—Beginners need sturdy chairs that have form-fitting seats and the necessary support for their shoulders. The height of the chairs should permit the feet to rest firmly on the floor. Chairs ten inches high usually meet the needs of most four-year-old children. Chairs twelve inches high are better suited to children five years old. If a uniform size is desired, it should be eleven inches. Teachers in the department will find chairs fourteen inches high satisfactory for their use. The secretary needs one of regular size, and either fourteen-inch chairs or those of regular size should be provided for visitors.

Tables—The average department will probably not need more than two tables, one for the book center, one for the work center, and a small tea table. The top of all tables should be ten inches higher than the seat of the chairs.

Where there is limited space folding tables may be used. They too should be sawed off to ten inches higher than the seat of the chairs. These may be folded up and put out of the way when the children come into the large group.

Tables built under a window or attached to the door may also be used where there is limited space.

For use in large group activities the superintendent-teacher needs a small table, twenty-one inches high, on which to place the department Bible, a vase of flowers, pictures, and other teaching materials.

The secretary should have a flattop desk or a table of regular size with sufficient drawer space to take care of her supplies.

A carpet or rugs.—If it is possible, a carpet or a large rug should be provided. It adds to the appearance of the room and the comfort of the children. When they build with blocks or engage in other play activities or assemble for a story, the children often sit on the floor. When they do, a rug also protects their clothing. If a carpet or a large rug cannot be provided, two or three small rugs can be used to advantage. They should always be kept clean, for this is necessary to the children's health.

PROVIDE FOR DEPARTMENT ACTIVITIES

A musical instrument, a cabinet for the safekeeping of supplies, and low shelves for the use of the children are three items of equipment that contribute in special ways to the promotion of department activities.

Piano.—The only satisfactory musical instrument for a Beginner department is a piano. A studio or spinet piano with a good tone makes a lovely choice. It should be kept tuned to concert pitch. Its position should make it easy for the pianist to co-operate with the superintendent-teacher as she guides the large group activities.

Cabinet.—Every well-ordered department needs a cabinet in which to care for teaching materials and other necessary supplies. The size and arrangement of the room should determine the dimensions of the cabinet, and whether a built-in or separate one is more desirable. Finishing the cabinet to match the woodwork and painting the shelves to match the furniture give a pleasing effect.

Open shelves.—Low open shelves approximately three and one-half feet high should be provided for each center of interest used on Sunday morning. There will be four or more centers of interest in operation every Sunday. These centers should be far enough apart to allow the children plenty of room in using the materials which they will find on the same shelves, in the same place every Sunday.

The size and shape of the room will determine the arrangement of the shelf units about the room.

CONTRIBUTE TO HOMELIKE ATMOSPHERE

The more homelike the room, the more at home children just venturing out from the home's protecting circle feel. The more beautiful it is in their eyes, the more they will love it and look forward to coming to it each Sunday.

Permanent pictures.—Well-chosen wall pictures are effective in creating the desired atmosphere. As the children come in Sunday after Sunday, they make friends with these pictures and experience satisfaction in finding them always in place.

A department needs two or perhaps four pictures, depending upon the size of the room and the size of the pictures. The following list suggests several choices that are especially appropriate:

Suffer Little Children, Tarrant
Christ Blessing Little Children, Plockhorst
Sistine Madonna, Raphael
Infant Samuel, Reynolds
Spring Song, Glucklich
We Give Thanks, Jessie Wilcox Smith
Twinkle, Twinkle, Little Star, Jessie Wilcox Smith

Such pictures are as truly teaching material as the teaching pictures provided for temporary use. They should hang flat against the wall, low enough for the children to see and touch. In a large room, an especially beautiful picture may be placed on a low, firmly built easel.

Draperies for windows.—Curtains or draperies add so much to the attractiveness and homelikeness of the department room that they are more than worth their cost and upkeep. They should not shut out light. Any materials used over the glass should be sheer, like theatrical gauze or marquisette. Effective draperies, with or without the sheer curtains, range from heavy unbleached domestic to a good quality of cretonne, or simple heavy silk materials. If the draperies are on cranes they can be swung out of the way when the children are at the windows.

ADJUSTING SMALL SCHOOL EQUIPMENT

The necessity for making adjustments in equipment is not confined to the small school. There are times when the problem is too much room, which makes adjustment vital to good work. Screens may be used to cut off excess floor space and thus make a more acceptable place for four- and five-year-olds. More often, however, the need for adjustment is found in schools where no provision was made for the children when the church building was erected.

USE AN AVAILABLE ROOM

In many churches of this kind there are two rooms, one on each side of the pulpit, used for dressing rooms when there is a baptismal service. Frequently these rooms become "catch-alls" for old literature, stoves, and useless things. Properly cleaned and redecorated, one of them will serve acceptably as a place for the Beginners without interfering with its intended use. Of course no illusion of the eye can increase the size of a room, but a larger appearance may be achieved by painting the woodwork to match the walls in a soft yellow or ivory tone and by hanging a large mirror on one wall.

SCREEN A CORNER

Sometimes a church realizes its need for a separate place for little children, but one corner of the church house is all it can provide at present. Such a corner forms two sides of a "room" and light beaverboard screens can be used to form the other two. These screens do not shut out sounds but they do shut out sights, and this is a great help in working with children.

Another way to arrange a separate place is to use curtains hung on wires strung about the space. These wires should be put up carefully and stretched tautly. Sagging curtains are most unsightly.

Unbleached sheeting makes cheap and satisfactory curtains. It launders easily, is not transparent and, like the beaverboard screens, forms a nice background for pictures and other decorations. Tabs sewed about six inches apart along the top of the curtains and the use of safety pins simplify attaching them to the wire. The tabs and pins also make it easy to take the curtains down when they need laundering or to push them against the wall when they have served their purpose for the day. The bottoms of the curtains should be ten or twelve inches from the floor. This allows the air to circulate and makes the "room" more comfortable.

IMPROVISE FURNITURE

In either the room or the screened corner, chairs are preferable for seats because they lend themselves more readily to informal arrangement. Split bottom chairs which are available in many communities meet the needs very nicely if they are the proper size. In lieu of chairs individual homemade stools or low benches seating four children make acceptable substitutes.

When limited space precludes the use of a regular table, a small folding one or a shelf hinged to the wall at the height of twenty inches may be used. Short lengths of chain may support the shelf when in use, and hooks may hold it in place against the wall when it is not needed.

Cabinets may be improvised from orange crates. One crate standing upright offers two shelves for supplies and a convenient place for a vase of flowers. Two crates placed one above the other lengthwise offer more shelf space. A bright curtain placed around them adds to the appearance of the cabinet and affords protection for the contents.

SELECTING TEACHING MATERIALS

There is a wealth of teaching materials and other department supplies from which the teachers may make selections. However, everything which they or the children use in the department should have real educational value for little children and should be suitable for use in their religious training.

SOUTHERN BAPTIST LITERATURE

The Baptist Sunday School Board knows the needs of Beginner teachers and pupils and makes available for them lesson materials and other helps of unexcelled quality. The special course of lessons for children four and five years of age is prepared by workers well versed in the Bible who have had large opportunity for studying the needs of small children and the ways in which they learn. It provides new lessons for every quarter and a Bible story for every Sunday. The following materials are provided for the teachers and the children:

Beginner Teacher.—This quarterly of forty-eight pages is designed especially to help Beginner teachers. In addition to the three-page treatment of each lesson in the quarter, it contains nine pages of helpful articles and seasonal suggestions. No teacher can do her best work without this special help in addition to the leaflet offered for the children.

Beginner Teaching Pictures.—Large and very beautiful teaching pictures are offered in quarterly sets. They are lithographed in four colors on durable cardboard, so that they may undergo much handling without undue damage. The *Beginner Teacher* suggests how teachers and children can use the pictures in connection with the lesson each Sunday.

Beginner Bible Story.—This four-page leaflet is for the children to take home each Sunday. It carries a picture in color, a Bible story, a verse for the children, and a message for the parents. The message is designed to help the parents tie up the Sunday school lesson with the children's home experiences.

Storytime.—Recognizing both the children's hunger for stories and the importance of giving them the right kind of stories during these days when tastes are being formed, the Baptist Sunday School Board publishes *Storytime,* a weekly paper. A copy should be given each child every Sunday in addition to his copy of the *Beginner Bible Story.* Parents and teachers will find it a real help and should enjoy reading the stories to the children as much as they enjoy hearing them.

Songbooks.—The fact that the children learn only a limited number of songs adds importance to the selection of songbooks. *Songs We Sing,* by Leatherwood, contains a collection of songs especially suited to the needs of Beginners. They cover a wide range of everyday experiences and express the thoughts of little children in language they can understand. The music is excellent and is well suited to the words. *Songs for the Pre-School Age,* by Shumate, is also a popular collection. The simple and tuneful songs deserve a place in every Beginner department.

The Sunday School Builder.—This magazine, which is published monthly by the Baptist Sunday School Board, carries helps for all Sunday school workers. Beside a wealth of material in other sections which Beginner teachers will find interesting and valuable, there is a section devoted exclusively to seasonal suggestions for them. The Sunday school should make the magazine available just as it does other teaching materials.

Department Bible.—This Bible contains thirty-three pictures which have been chosen from the teaching pictures of the Nursery, Beginner, and Primary departments.

RECORD MATERIALS

Good records are vital to good work. The well-known Six Point Record System is adapted for the Beginner department and its use is necessary to good records. Forms are offered to meet every need. The following list is suggestive:

> Classification Slips, Form 10
> Pupil Enrolment Cards, Form 20
> Class Record Card, Form 35E
> Report of Department Secretary, Form 40
> Monthly Report of Department, Form 100A
> Class Book for Beginners, No. 8
> Department Secretary's Record, No. 2
> Absentee Report Slip, Form AR-1
> Weekly Visitation Slip, Form VR-1

The Class Book for Beginners, No. 8, is for the teacher. It enables her to have the record of her children for consultation at any time. She should not leave it at the Sunday school but take it home.

All other materials are for the school. The department secretary in co-operation with the general secretary is responsible for their safekeeping.

HANDWORK MATERIALS

Rightly used, handwork has real value as an educational activity. The children find it fascinating and participate wholeheartedly in types suited to their abilities, such as drawing, cutting, and simple pasting. For these activities the department needs an assortment of materials. The following are suggestive:

> Drawing paper cut in several sizes
> Construction paper in assorted colors
> Blunt scissors
> Large crayons
> Paste and paste spreaders
> Small pictures
> Cardboard for posters
> Blank scrapbooks
> Bird and flower stickers

BOOKS AND PICTURES

Suitable books and pictures with which the children make friends not only give pleasure but also serve as valuable teaching material. There should be books which the teachers may read to the children, books whose pictures tell their own stories, and books whose pictures invite conversation about God's love and care, and about kindness, helpfulness, and obedience. Attractive and durable bindings invite the children to look within and enable them to use the books without tearing them.

PLAY EQUIPMENT

Play is now recognized as one of the God-given ways in which children learn most easily. Not every plaything is suitable for use in Sunday school but there are a number that are valuable in developing appreciations, in helping the children to share, to take turns, and to practice other desirable conduct.

Blocks.—The importance of blocks justifies giving them first place in the list of desirable play equipment. They not only make an unusual appeal to the children but also hold their interests for long periods of time and lend themselves to many different uses.

A good carpenter can make acceptable blocks for a department by using lightweight wood and sandpapering it to eliminate splinters. There is no rule regarding the sizes, but the following are satisfactory:

Bricks	Cubes	Columns	Boards
2x4x4″	2″	2x2x4″	4x12x1″
2x4x6″	5″	2x2x6″	4x18x1″
2x4x8″		2x2x8″	8x 8x1″

For a group of fifty children, fifty bricks, fifteen cubes, ten columns, and six boards of each size may be provided. Ten bricks of each size cut diagonally will stimulate the imagination of the children as they use the blocks in building. Round columns may be substituted for the square ones listed.

Toys.—There is no place in a department for mechanical toys or others designed merely for entertainment. The collection should include only those which can be used to create situations in which desired learnings may take place. For example, housekeeping toys are popular alike with boys and girls. Dolls with well-made clothing that children take off and put on and take off again are especially desirable. Doll beds, carriages, dishes, and other items that suggest everyday experiences give opportunity for helping the children to appreciate what others do and what they themselves can do to make the home happy. They afford opportunity also for helping them to recognize the rights of other children, to share and take turns, and thus live happily with one another. The use of play equipment like the use of other teaching materials should tie in with the plans for the session.

CHAPTER OUTLINE

GIVING THE BIBLE ITS RIGHTFUL PLACE
  Recognize It as God's Book
  Develop Appreciations

ARRANGING MATERIALS IN CENTERS OF INTEREST
  Invite Experiences in Seeing and Touching
  Stimulate Interest in Pictures and Books
  Encourage Purposive Handwork
  Suggest Play Activities

ENGAGING IN EDUCATIVE ENTERPRISES
  Create Readiness
  Give Guidance in Planning
  Carry Plans to Completion
  Talk Over Results

TAKING TRIPS AND NATURE WALKS
HELPING THE CHILDREN TO REST AND RELAX

CHAPTER IV

USING MATERIALS AND ACTIVITIES

From the wealth of materials available for work with Beginners and the many activities which promise enriching experiences, teachers should select those best suited to their particular situations. It is important also that they give careful thought to the use of these materials and activities to bring about desired results in the lives of the children.

GIVING THE BIBLE ITS RIGHTFUL PLACE

The material that is first in importance and to which the teachers should give most careful attention is the Bible. It is the textbook of the Sunday school and while it was not written directly for four- and five-year-olds, it is adequate to meet all their life needs as well as the life needs of their teachers and parents.

> There's just one Book for the tender years—
> One Book alone for guiding
> The little feet through the joys and fears
> That unknown days are hiding.
> There's just one Book.
>
> —Selected

Recognize It as God's Book

By their attitude, as well as through precept and example, teachers should help the children to recognize the Bible as God's Book. They should begin early to nurture respect for its authority.

The Bible which is provided for the department should be an especially beautiful one, illustrated with colored pictures. It should be placed regularly where the children can see and handle it. The teachers should not only take advantage of occasions that arise but should also make opportunities to use it.

Because the children are living now and need God and God's help to solve the problems they meet every day, the Bible material which is used with them should be chosen with their present needs and capacities in mind. There should also be earnest endeavor on the part of the teachers to help the children make a natural connection between the teaching of a Bible story, verse, or passage and their own needs and problems. As an illustration, the teachers should help them to feel that the same God who showed Baby Moses' mother how to care for him helps other mothers, even the Beginners' own, to care for their little ones in definite ways.

Often before she tells a story a teacher may find it natural to say, "That reminds me of a lovely story which we find in God's Book." Or it may be after a story she may say quietly and without artificiality: "That was a story Jesus told. We find it here in God's Book." Many times the opportunity is offered for her to make such observations as: "I know because God's Book tells me so," or "We must mind our mothers and daddies because God's Book says we should."

DEVELOP APPRECIATIONS

In addition to helping the children recognize the Bible as God's Book, all earnest teachers want to help them think of it as "God's dear Book," filled with beautiful verses and stories which tell of God and Jesus and show children what to do. They want to help them to love the Book as well as to respect and obey it.

That the children may develop these appreciations, certain ways of using the Bible and Bible material are suggested.

Talk and sing about the Bible.—Teachers should speak often of God's goodness in giving the Bible to the people and of how people have loved it and been helped through reading it. They should speak also of how it should be picked up and put down and should set examples in its reverent handling. Frequently they may let the children show one another how the Book should be handled and allow them to hold it while the group sings songs about it. The teachers should examine with interest the Bibles which the Beginners themselves bring.

They should also find ways for using the Bibles that are brought. For example, they may read from them, let the children place their hands on the verse for the day, and find pictures appropriate to the lesson emphasis. Such experiences make the children happy and encourage them to associate the Bible with God's house and all that goes on there.

Five-year-old James whose custom it was to bring his Bible every Sunday appeared one morning with a slip of paper and a special request. He said: "I want this paper put in my Bible where it says, 'God loveth a cheerful giver.' My mother knows it's in the Bible, but we want to know where." The teacher marked the place for him and to his great delight read the verse from his Bible during the offering service. This experience led her to mark the places of favorite verses in the Bibles of other children. For markers she prepared lengths of ribbons in several colors which she placed in the Bibles in addition to marking the verses lightly with pencil.

Use Bible stories and verses.—Familiar Bible stories should be often recalled in touch-and-go fashion as a part of the conversation and for meeting various situations that arise.

Verses of Scripture should also be blended into the procedure. Although Beginners can and do learn the actual words of the Bible, which are a part of their lesson material, they learn them through natural use and not through drill. Sometimes, for instance, in working out a service project, a teacher says conversationally, "We love him, because he first loved us." When beautiful outdoor things are examined, she brings "He hath made every thing beautiful in his time," into the give and take of ideas. In like manner, she uses verses about the sunshine, rain, snow, and wind as part of the discussion when they suit the weather.

There are occasions when longer passages may be brought into the procedure just as naturally. Reading Luke 2:8-16, for example, proves effective as a recall the Sunday after the story has been told. Sometimes a dramatic setting can be made. This was done by a teacher who brought into a discussion of what families do on Christmas Eve the custom of reading Bible passages by the light of a candle sent into the home by the department. The group then played "Christmas Eve" and gathered about the "Daddy's" knee (the teacher being "Daddy") to hear God's Book tell about the first Christmas.

The teachers should always be careful to select passages that have real meaning for the children. The following are suggestive: Genesis 1:1-5; Genesis 1:24-25; Psalm 104:10-14; Song of Solomon 2:11-12; Matthew 13:3-8; Matthew 2:1-5; and Matthew 2:8-11.

In her book *Experiences in the Church School Kindergarten*, Jessie Eleanor Moore suggests combining Bible verses into "thought wholes" for reading to the children. The following selections are appropriate for use in this way:

At our gates are all manner of pleasant fruits (Song of Sol. 7:13). Unto thee, O God, do we give thanks (Psalm 75:1).

He giveth snow like wool (Psalm 147:16). The lambs are for thy clothing (Prov. 27:26). Unto thee, O God, do we give thanks (Psalm 75:1).

The birds of the air have nests (Matt. 8:20). [They] sing among the branches (Psalm 104:12). Your heavenly Father feedeth them (Matt. 6:26). Unto thee, O God, do we give thanks (Psalm 75:1).

✓ *Dramatize Bible stories.*—Some stories, such as David's care of the sheep, lend themselves to dramatization as a whole. Only certain portions of other stories should be dramatized. The life of Samuel in the tabernacle, which gives patterns of helpfulness, for example, may be played out, but the play should not continue until Samuel hears God speak to him. God, the Father, and Jesus should never be dramatized, though the truth of stories or parts of stories about Jesus are quite suitable for dramatization.

ARRANGING MATERIALS IN CENTERS OF INTEREST

Although a very definite time is set for Sunday school to begin, it is a recognized fact that for every child it begins when he arrives. Finding something interesting with which he can immediately work or play not only makes him happy but also affords opportunity for desirable learning experiences. In keeping with the teaching emphasis of the day, materials may be used to form centers of interest about which the children may gather in small groups. Each child should be allowed to choose the activity that appeals to his interest and should feel free to move from one center to another, but the teachers should be ready to give needed help and guidance.

INVITE EXPERIENCES IN SEEING AND TOUCHING

Among the suitable objects which can be used to invite experiences in seeing and touching are fresh flowers, autumn leaves, winter evergreen, flower seed, and seed pods—anything which speaks of God's creative power and the rhythm of the seasons. The homes of birds and other creatures, such as used birds' nests, mud daubers' houses, and shells arouse thoughts of God's wise provision of a home for each living thing.

Pine cones, smooth pebbles, and other objects which are considered just "pretty," as well as those which are useful for food or clothing, all have a place in teaching about God's goodness in providing everything beautiful and needful.

Suppose the desired outcome for the day is to give the children an understanding and appreciation of how God makes provision for their food, and the lesson plans include the use of the story of Ruth gleaning in the field of Boaz. The teachers may find it helpful to arrange a center of interest of beautifully formed fruit and vegetables which are suitable for the children's food. Oranges, apples, carrots, and tomatoes, which may be sensed through smell, as well as through sight and touch, are especially appealing. As the children gather about the center, they may engage in conversation, use Bible verses, and spontaneously sing familiar songs. Such experiences, if wisely guided, should lead to a real "Thank you, dear God, for our food," and to an intelligent, appreciative background for the story.

When teaching that God permits people to help him care for his lesser creatures, teachers may bring a rabbit, a basket of young puppies, or a canary into the department. A careful handling of these little creatures and feeding them, too, if practical, afford real experience in being helpful. Such teaching is better than "much speaking."

Such materials as replicas of an Oriental house and the children's own church building may also be used helpfully as centers of interest.

Beginners enjoy building Oriental houses and modern churches of blocks, but sometimes there are needs for cardboard or other replicas for handling and examining in order to clarify ideas. Through the use of replicas, Elisha's room on the roof, the type of home in which the boy Jesus lived, and the lowering of the paralytic through the roof can be made clearer to the children.

A replica of the local church may be used effectively as a center of interest in a unit of lessons about God's house. Paper doll families may represent the actual Beginner families as the children play. The thought of behavior suitable in God's house may be brought into the conversation as well as how the love gifts of grandparents, parents, and perhaps the children themselves helped to build and are helping to keep the real church.

STIMULATE INTEREST IN PICTURES AND BOOKS

Pictures and books should be displayed where the children can look at them and handle them readily. Placed on the picture rail before the children arrive, pictures arouse interest in the problem that the session is to solve or help tie up the experiences of a unit of lessons. It is sometimes desirable to leave each Sunday's lesson pictures on the rail until a series is formed. Beginners find it interesting to examine this growing center and to recall the stories the pictures suggest.

On other occasions the use of a single picture brings gratifying results. One group seemed almost to relive the story of Jesus blessing little children when all other pictures were removed and a very large copy of *Jesus and Children* was placed on a low easel.

Although the teachers should tell and not read the lesson story which is introduced as a part of the morning's procedure, there is a very definite place for the story which they do read. Often the soft voice of a teacher reading from a book of their choice gives the children confidence when they first arrive at Sunday school.

Beginners also enjoy gathering about a browsing table on which there are books with special interest appeal. Examining the books frequently results in the request, "Read me about this." Again it leads to conversation and the sharing of experiences related to the teaching emphasis for the day.

ENCOURAGE PURPOSIVE HANDWORK

Through choice beforehand and by direct and indirect suggestion, teachers should see that all handwork is purposive. For instance, the idea that one can pray at any time and any place was strengthened for the members of one group when they completed a poster on which the teacher had placed a picture of the *Infant Samuel*, by Reynolds. Selecting from a number which had been previously cut out by the teacher, they added pictures of children and grownups at prayer—saying grace at the table, praying at church, praying singly and in groups. When the poster was finished, they placed it on the picture rail to help make the room pretty and to serve as a silent reminder that God always listens when one calls upon him.

Similarly the making of scrapbooks and puzzles for the sick, the assembling of leaflets for absentees, and the making of valentines and other gifts for home people or playmates are types of purposive handwork. These are real experiences in showing love to others as Jesus would have his people do.

SUGGEST PLAY ACTIVITIES

The interest of the Beginners in their blocks, dolls, furniture, and other playthings leads to activities which are among the most valuable of their learning experiences. Blocks invite them to build a church, the homes of people, and roads going to the church, and thus create situations in which it is natural to use songs, stories, and

Bible verses. Dolls suggest playing "Mother," "keeping house," "visiting and being visited," and other home activities which develop appreciations and give opportunity for conduct patterns. Dishes encourage working together as preparations are made for a meal and the giving of thanks as the children talk about the good gifts God's love provides.

ENGAGING IN EDUCATIVE ENTERPRISES

The value of an enterprise depends largely upon its choice and the tactful guidance of the teachers in making the selection. Four- and five-year-olds should not be expected to get religious training, for example, from sharing with those with whom they have no contact or in whom they have no interest. Nor should sharing be with the vague "poor." There should be a real reason why the particular group should share with the chosen group—a reason all the members can feel. The needs and preferences of the recipients should always be considered.

Perhaps the one with whom the group purposes to share needs songs more than a basket of food or a basket of groceries more than one of beautiful fruit. The enterprise, too, should bring satisfaction to the children themselves. Into any sharing enterprise which they carry through there should be woven the thought that by showing love to others they are showing love for Jesus who loves all people everywhere and wants them to be happy.

CREATE READINESS

The first step in connection with any enterprise is to get the children ready to enter into it wholeheartedly. They need guidance in recognizing a need and responding to it until they have enough experiences through practice to think for themselves of things they can do. Even so, they can often exercise real choice in planning their projects. This was done by a group to whom the teacher read a letter from a council of Sunday school leaders telling of various services needed at Christmas-time. Talking it over with their teachers, the children chose as their service enterprise the making of small Christmas trees to be used on the trays of little folks in a hospital, being influenced no doubt by the fact that one of their number must spend Christmas there. Having chosen it themselves, they naturally were much interested in carrying it through.

GIVE GUIDANCE IN PLANNING

Usually the children need guidance in the making of plans. When it was decided that the teachers should bring the trees and the children the gifts, the first reaction of the children was to bring gifts too heavy for the trees. When a teacher explained that the trees would be very small and showed them how small, they changed their plans accordingly. The question of how to secure parent co-operation was raised at this time. The teachers had anticipated it, of course, and had material ready for the explanatory notes which the children helped to make and carried home with them.

CARRY PLANS TO COMPLETION

Children should be allowed to execute their plans. In this, too, the teachers may make needed suggestions and give encouragement, but if the work is suited to the abilities of Beginners, the joy of doing it should be theirs. The trees used in the enterprise described were set firmly erect in small flower pots filled with sand. On two Sundays the children worked in small groups and wrapped the pots in tin foil. Both the "gifts" brought from the homes and those bought with contributed money were tied to the trees in single knots. Tinsel icicles and decorations fashioned by placing two star stickers together over the end of the limbs made the trees very attractive.

TALK OVER RESULTS

The finished work should be a source of satisfaction to the children. Those who prepared the trees thought they were "pretty" and found pleasure in sending them on their mission. One child made a special request that John, the Beginner child in the hospital, be given the one she had made.

Since the situation prevented the children from carrying out this part of the enterprise, a teacher delivered the trees. At this point, as always, judgment must be exercised by the teachers. For instance, a number of the children may slip into the church to leave a lily for the pastor if a helper is responsible for each group of five or six, but an automobile trip to a hospital is not practical for a large group of young children.

Further evaluation took place the following Sunday when the teacher who delivered the gifts gave a report of their reception. By that time, too, a letter had arrived from the hospital which, when read to the children, gave them the feeling that their effort had been worth while. One child said, "Let's make them some more trees."

TAKING TRIPS AND NATURE WALKS

Lesson material sometimes suggests taking the group into the church auditorium, visiting shut-ins, and going out-of-doors to see what beautiful things can be found.

The elements of time and suitability should always be considered in the use of such activities. There may be time during a Sunday school session, for example, to deepen appreciation of God's house through a visit to the auditorium, where the children hear the organist play some of their favorite songs, and hear the pastor read from God's Word and speak to God in prayer. There may be time for the group to go around the corner or across the street to share songs and stories with a shut-in, but a trip that would consume all the Sunday school hour would be suitable very rarely.

Trips to the baker's or the florist's, and similiar activities, valuable because they are a part of a sharing project or because they give information about community helpers, should be weekday excursions. Trips to the woods and parks are suitable on weekdays or Sunday afternoons and are especially appropriate in connection with Vacation Bible school work.

Any trip planned for Beginners should have a definite place in the program of activities and should be carefully supervised so that it will contribute to their religious development.

A nature walk is always a happy excursion. Firsthand experiences with the things God has made, and is making, is always better than hearing them talked about, seeing pictures of them, or even examining them after they are brought into the room. Suburban and country churches are usually so situated that children can step out in the churchyard to see how the sun has helped the lilacs bloom or to check up on the growth of the bulbs or the seeds they have planted. When under the teacher's guidance, the children discover a bird's nest, sense the strength of the spring wind and see it sweeping the earth clean for springtime awakening, they may be brought into close companionship with God, the Creator and the Lawgiver.

HELPING THE CHILDREN TO REST AND RELAX

Provision should be made to avoid and to relieve bodily tension without the need for rest being mentioned. Singing may be used before handwork becomes tiring. Representative play, which may be a response to rhythm or playing "nighttime," as the children rest their heads on their arms, finds great favor with four- and five-year-olds and is very effective as relaxation. Listening for certain things in quiet instrumental music also helps children to rest and relax and prepares them to go on with profit to the next activity.

CHAPTER OUTLINE

Using Instrumental Music

Creating Mood
Helping to Interpret Mood
Promoting Orderliness

Selecting Beginner Songs

Considering Children's Experiences
Examining the Words of a Song
Giving Careful Thought to Music

Using Beginner Songs

Teaching New Songs
Making Familiar Through Repetition
Meeting Program Needs

CHAPTER V

TEACHING THROUGH MUSIC AND SONG

The seventeenth century poet who said, "Music hath charms," was not thinking in terms of little children. Nevertheless, the statement may be fittingly applied to them. Early in life they begin to manifest a desire for musical experience. "Pat-a-cake, pat-a-cake, baker-man," which is one of their earliest accomplishments, is a response to rhythm. Even before they reach Beginner age they are singing tiny songs, and frequently the songs are of their own making.

Sometimes their original songs describe an activity in which they are engaged. "I'm sweeping the floor, I'm sweeping the floor," sang a small boy as he followed his mother and used his broom as nearly as he could like she used hers. Again the songs give expression to some desire or to an experience of happiness.

Mrs. Aurora Shumate tells of a child who, as she stood before the mirror helping herself to her mother's creams and powder, sang to a bright little tune: "I'm so nervous! I'm so nervous!" The fact that the words were borrowed and were beyond the child's understanding did not dampen her ardor as she gave expression to the gladness that filled her heart.

Understanding parents recognize the importance of giving encouragement to their little children's apprecia-tion of music and their efforts to sing. They not only make it possible for the little ones to hear beautiful music in the home but also often find time to sing for them and with them.

Beginner teachers should also recognize the value of music in the lives of the children. Instrumental music and the singing of songs make specific contributions to their religious nurture, and blessed are they for whom a church provides a good piano and a capable, consecrated, sympathetic pianist.

USING INSTRUMENTAL MUSIC

There are many ways in which instrumental music may be used advantageously with the children. It is particularly valuable, however, in creating mood, helping to interpret mood, and promoting orderliness.

CREATING MOOD

One day two small boys, sons of foreign-born parents, stood in front of a great church in a Southern city. "There it is!" said one of them, "that's my church! There's a big organ in it and the music makes me feel all good inside."

The use of carefully chosen instrumental music helps Beginners to feel "all good inside." At times it speaks to them in quiet tones and calls them to reverence and prayer. Again it speaks to them in bright, joyous tones and causes them to rejoice and be glad.

HELPING TO INTERPRET MOOD

Instrumental music is also effective in helping the children to find expression for their feelings in the clapping of hands loudly or softly, swaying, skipping, and walking lightly or with heavy tread. Many forms of representative play are made more enjoyable as the children catch the rhythm of suitable music and become fluttering leaves, kittens with cushioned feet, or birds that fly gracefully about the room.

PROMOTING ORDERLINESS

Instrumental music in the department helps also to promote orderliness. The children soon learn to respond readily when the piano speaks to them from time to time, asking them to put away their toys, to assemble in a large group, to play more quietly, or to speak more softly.

The "stand up" and "sit down" chords, which formerly played an important part in the procedure, are no longer used every time it is desirable to have the children stand or be seated. Occasionally, however, it may be helpful to use them.

SELECTING BEGINNER SONGS

Music makes its largest contribution to the work as accompaniment to songs. Always the songs should be carefully selected as many which are offered are unsuited for four- and five-year-olds. In making the selections, the teachers should give consideration to the children's limited experience. They should examine the words of the song and give careful thought to the accompanying music.

CONSIDERING CHILDREN'S EXPERIENCES

Because the interests of Beginners are largely centered in their homes, they like to sing about experiences they have there. The loving care of fathers and mothers, the part children can have in making home happy, their pets, and their playmates are themes for many well-loved songs. As they come to recognize everyday helpers, it is natural for them to want to sing about them, too, and the following song offers excellent opportunity:

> A helper kind and good,
> A helper kind and good,
> The postman is a friend of mine,
> A helper kind and good.[1]

The third line is easily adapted to fit the occasion if the children wish to express appreciation for the farmer,

---

[1] *Songs We Sing* (Nashville: Broadman Press, 1939), p. 22.

the milkman, the doctor, or another who ministers to their happiness and welfare.

Beginners feel a kinship with trees and flowers and birds. Their vivid imagination enables them to personify these friends and thrill to such messages as:

> The trees in their new dresses,
> The little birds that sing,
> And all the buds and blossoms
> Say, "God has sent the spring."[2]

The children's ideas of God are being formed as much, if not more, by the songs they sing and to which they listen than by the words they hear in conversation or story. To preclude their getting erroneous ideas, their limited experiences should have careful consideration in choosing their songs.

Mention has been made of the difficulty children of this age find in symbolism, which is no less confusing to them in a song than in a picture or a story. They love the first stanza of "Jesus Loves Me," but there are two reasons why they cannot appreciate the other stanzas. First, they introduce symbolism and, second, they mention experiences which cannot be explained to little children.

Beginner songs should be short. Four lines is a good length for a stanza, and one stanza is usually enough for a song unless there is much repetition in the succeeding stanzas. The repetition not only appeals to the children but also helps them to learn the song more readily.

EXAMINING THE WORDS OF A SONG

Some songs which are offered for little children are unsuited to their use because the words are beyond their understanding. The vocabulary of an individual child is often surprisingly large, but the common vocabulary

---

[2] *Songs We Sing* (Nashville: Broadman Press, 1939), p. 34.

of any given group of children is limited. Unless a song expresses their thoughts in language which they can understand, to sing it will confuse rather than help them.

In other songs the words have no religious value, and the rhyme is forced. The words of every song chosen for Beginners should be simple but wholesome. It is not necessary or even desirable for every song to contain words of praise or prayer but it should at least contribute to desirable appreciations and conduct.

Occasionally someone questions the religious value of a song like the following, which the children find delight in singing:

> The daisy in her ruffled cap,
>   Is always good to see, . . .
> She nods like this, she nods like that,
>   And sweetly smiles at me.[3]

"Perhaps," says Elizabeth McEwen Shields, "we can best answer this question by showing how a song may contribute to a religious experience even though it does not in itself express ideas that are specifically religious. A certain type of song may be a delightful medium for giving information—almost a part of a conversation— enlarging a child's world so that when he is guided to connect God with this world his experience is truly religious.

"You will remember that Jesus had his disciples *consider* the lilies of the field before he connected God with the experience. And our Saviour's word picture is so vivid that down through the years the royal robes of the field lilies have found a place in poetry, music, and art. Then this vivid picture was made a part of a religious experience. 'Wherefore,' he said, 'if God so clothe the grass of the field, which to day is, and to morrow is

[3] *Songs We Sing* (Nashville: Broadman Press, 1939), p. 38.

cast into the oven, shall he not much more clothe you, O ye of little faith?" (Matt. 6:30).

"Thus a song like 'The Daisy' may help little children to 'consider,' may stimulate and lend variety to conversation that may bring a religious response, voiced or unvoiced."

Beginners like glad songs. There is no place in their lives for solemn words or music. The songs they love best often include the words "I am glad" or "I am happy."

One morning a Beginner teacher placed within easy reach of her group a picture of children skipping in a circle, clapping their hands, and singing. Immediately upon seeing it, a four-year-old took possession of it. She placed the picture upright in one chair and sat in another facing it to enjoy the picture all by herself. The teacher watched her for a few minutes and then drew near to ask, "Do you like the picture?"

"Oh, yes!" said the child, "they are singing:

> We're glad today, we're glad today,
> For the sunshine we're glad today, . . ."

The teacher caught her enthusiasm and entering into tne experience, sang the last line with her:

> Thank Thee, God in heaven.[4]

GIVING CAREFUL THOUGHT TO MUSIC

During these early years the children are forming their taste for music, and only the best should be offered them. It should always interpret and enrich the words of a song. Joyous words should be accompanied by joyous music, and words of prayer should be sung to a quiet, reverent melody.

[4]*Songs for the Pre-School Age* (Nashville: Broadman Press, 1939), p. 24.

The range of Beginner voices is another matter for consideration. Some authorities suggest, "Keep on the staff." Others feel that an occasional D below the staff is acceptable. All agree that the children should be encouraged to use very light head tones in their singing. A simple melody with light harmony, which allows the melody to stand out clearly, should invite them to sing with joy and abandon unconscious of effort.

USING BEGINNER SONGS

The songs should be used naturally just as are conversation and stories. At any time while the children are working and playing in small groups, a teacher may sing to them or encourage them to sing with her about some experience they are enjoying. The flowers a child brings to make God's house beautiful may suggest a song about the flowers or one about God's house and God's day.

As the children arrange the flowers in a vase and bring water to keep them fresh, the teacher may frequently sing casually but effectively a song about helping.

It is not even necessary to announce a song with which the children are familiar when introducing it into the procedure of the large group. The pianist may play a few measures or the superintendent-teacher may begin to sing and the pianist follow. In this way the song will fit smoothly into the conversation or follow naturally the story or the use of Bible verses.

TEACHING NEW SONGS

"That reminds me of a song," is often sufficient reason for the superintendent-teacher to sing a new song which she wishes the group to learn. She should sing it without accompaniment and pronounce the words very distinctly. It is important that she sing the words instead of speaking them for the words and tune should make their impression together. Later she may sing the song with piano accompaniment and invite the group to sing with her. It will be all right for her to use the song several times during the session if opportunity is offered. Always in presenting the song she should sing all of a stanza or the entire song just as she would show all of a picture before calling attention to a special part of it.

If a song introduces words or experiences that are new to the children, the teacher should develop it before she sings it. Through the use of pictures, incident stories, or the recall of experiences, she may explain and clarify new words and expressions. Then the children will understand and appreciate them when they hear them in the song.

It is helpful for the children to sing the words without accompaniment as this gives the teacher an opportunity to discover and correct any mistakes they make in words or tune. A small boy went home from Sunday school one day and astonished his parents by singing lustily a song he had learned that morning. In the song the Bible verse, "Sing unto him, sing praises," was repeated several times, and every time the words "sing praises" occurred, the boy sang "He's crazy."

In another department the children had just learned a glad song in which the words "sweet hosannas" appeared. They liked the song and sang it so sweetly the superintendent-teacher stopped singing to listen to them. She was surprised to find that they were singing "sweet bananas" instead of "sweet hosannas."

Mistakes of this kind are to be expected when the children try to sing songs containing words beyond their comprehension. All too often, however, teachers overlook the fact that a word or phrase quite within the understanding of Beginners may be entirely new to them, and that failure to explain it may rob the song of its meaning.

Sometimes the children may be asked to listen while the piano "sings" the song, and the teacher calls attention to the way it "sings" a word or a phrase with which they find difficulty.

The music may be used as a march or a relaxation exercise to familiarize the children with it in advance of its use with the words.

MAKING FAMILIAR THROUGH REPETITION

Knowing a song well is necessary to the enjoyment of the children in singing it, but the teacher should not try to help them make the words their own through mechanical drill or through teaching a line at a time. Rather in singing the song for them she should enunciate the words very distinctly and then make them familiar through repetition. In learning a song, as well as when they know and love it, the children may enjoy singing it several times during one session.

In one department a group was welcoming a four-year-old who had been absent several Sundays on account of illness. The superintendent-teacher placed an arm around the child as she spoke of how they had missed him and of how they had often talked to the Heavenly Father about him. At this moment a little girl said, "Let's sing 'The Heavenly Father Cares for Me.'" Without further suggestion the group sang:

> The heav'nly Father cares for me,
>   Ev'ry, ev'ry day;
> I know He cares for you and you,
>   In the same, same way.[5]

The children were then asked to close their eyes and give opportunity for a birthday child to take the seat

[5] *Songs for the Pre-School Age* (Nashville: Broadman Press, 1939), p. 16.

of honor in a prettily decorated chair. When they opened their eyes and found the chair occupied, they wanted to repeat the song and did so with great enthusiasm.

As a relaxation activity the children took a walk in an imaginary park. There they found beautiful leaves, acorns, and other gifts about which to exclaim. Finally one child discovered an imaginary squirrel in the door of his imaginary home and called his friends to see. Soon they were singing again, "The Heavenly Father Cares for Me."

Later the teacher told the story of Elijah at the brook Cherith. The children listened eagerly as she told how God sent the ravens with bread and meat in the morning and with bread and meat in the evening. When the story ended, it was only natural that they should want to sing again "The Heavenly Father Cares for Me."

MEETING PROGRAM NEEDS

Singing may be used to meet various needs in the Sunday morning program. Perhaps no other activity is as effective for socializing a group. When the children sing together, a feeling of unity results which makes it easy for them to work and play together happily.

Songs also help to promote friendliness. The heart of even a timid child rejoices when his mates sing all for him:

> How do you do, how do you do,
>   How do you do today?
> We'll wave our hands and smile at you;
>   How do you do today?[6]

In like manner the singing of a birthday song brings happiness both to the birthday child and to the children who sing it.

[6]*Songs We Sing* (Nashville: Broadman Press, 1939), p. 19.

Five years old, five years old,
  Five years old today,
We'll sing our happy birthday song;
Jack's five years old today.

Tra-la-la, tra-la-la,
  Tra-la-la-la-la,
We'll sing our happy birthday song;
Jack's five years old today.[7]

Seasonal songs are especially valuable in developing appreciations, but program needs do not require that the children learn all that are used in the department. The teachers may sing to them some of the lovely ones whose usefulness is limited to a special day or season. Other songs of this type can be adjusted to different special days or seasons by changing a word or line. In this way a birthday greeting song may become a New Year or a Christmas greeting song, and a spring song may become a fall or winter song. The following is a good example of the latter type:

The winter has gone,
  The springtime is here;
And ev'rything tells me
  God . . . is near.[7]

The adaptability of this song is obvious, and because it so frequently meets a program need, the children come to know it well and find real happiness in singing it.

The purpose of some songs is to give information. They tell where the baby Jesus was born, who made the moon and stars so bright, and how Jesus put his hands on little children and prayed. There are other songs whose chief purpose is to teach Bible truths and suggest ways of acting that are pleasing to God. They tie in with the teaching emphasis of a program and are frequently

[7] *Songs We Sing* (Nashville: Broadman Press. 1939), p. 43.

referred to as theme songs. "The Heavenly Father Cares for Me" and "Jesus Loves Me," previously mentioned in this chapter, are of this type. "God's Book" and "The Happy Way," in *Songs We Sing*, are also examples.

Rarely, if ever, will all the types mentioned be needed in connection with the program for a given Sunday. Choices must be made and they should be governed by the purpose of the lesson and the preference of members of the group.

The loftiest purpose for which songs are used in the department is to give praise unto the Lord. This will be discussed in a later chapter but is mentioned here to emphasize the importance of using this type of song every Sunday.

Long ago following the triumphal entry of Jesus into Jerusalem, children followed the crowd of people into the temple and even there continued to sing:

Hosanna to the Son of David

The sound of their young voices was not pleasing to the scribes and the priests, and they besought Jesus to rebuke the children and have the singing stopped. But Jesus answering said, "Have ye never read, Out of the mouth of babes and sucklings thou hast perfected praise?" (Matt. 21:16).

Through the centuries since, children of many tribes and tongues have brought their tributes of love and praise to Jesus in song and have felt the sweetness of his presence and his blessing.

It is the privilege of Beginner teachers to help the children find God in the blue of the skies, the brightness of the sunshine, the beauty of the flowers, and the bounty of other blessings they enjoy. It is their privilege also to help them find in song a satisfying outlet for gratitude and praise.

> I am not satisfied to say
> "Thank you" when I kneel to pray
> For all around me everywhere
> There is so much to show God's care;
> So many good gifts I can see
> That whisper of his love for me,
> I want to run and sing and shout,
> And let my happy thoughts come out.
>
> —M. C. L.

CHAPTER OUTLINE

PROVIDING FOR WORSHIP EXPERIENCES

Planning in Advance
Putting the Room in Readiness
Making Personal Preparation

DEVELOPING AN AWARENESS OF GOD

Directing Conversation
Telling Stories
Showing Pictures
Reading Bible Verses

CONTRIBUTING TO QUIET WONDER

Using Instrumental Music
Considering Gifts of Nature

EXPRESSING WORSHIP IN SONG

Choosing Familiar Songs
Singing Original Songs

LEADING TO WORSHIPFUL PRAYER

Encouraging Spontaneous Prayer
Training in Prayer Expression

GUIDING IN WORSHIPFUL GIVING

CHAPTER VI

LEADING BEGINNERS TO WORSHIP

Beginner teachers have no greater privilege and no more delicate task than leading the children to worship. The consciousness of the reality of God—the feeling that God's presence is related to all the activities of life—is one of the richest gifts the children find in God's house.

PROVIDING FOR WORSHIP EXPERIENCES

Worship is most real to the children when it is related to their everyday living. They do not worship unless something stirs worshipful feelings in their hearts. They cannot, like grownups, recall previous experiences with enough vividness to feel God's presence anew.

For this reason, plans for the department session should be so flexible that whenever the children feel an impulse to worship they may do so. The impulse may come in connection with various experiences and at any time during the session. Regardless of when it comes, the teachers should recognize and use their opportunity to help the children express their love, or praise, or gratitude.

As an illustration, one Beginner group had made a cocoon tree. The children had helped to tie the cocoons to a branch of a tree and had placed the branch in a sunny window. They had carefully moistened the cocoons and had talked about them from time to time. Their teacher hoped that a moth would hatch at an opportune moment to help them sense God's miracle of quickening life at springtime.

The first moth made his appearance unexpectedly, however. Arriving early one Sunday morning, the

teacher discovered a beautiful velvet-like creature dry-
ing its wings on the curtain, after having left his snug
cradle by means of a tiny hole. "What a choice experience this promises for the large group period!" she
thought. "I will adjust my plans and give opportunity
for the children to examine the cocoon and the moth."

Soon the children began to arrive. Among the first
was Fred, a rough little redheaded fellow, who had been
the leader in caring for the cocoons. He was quick to
notice that there was a hole in one of them. "Did he
come out?" he asked excitedly as other children crowded
around to see.

The discovery brought disappointment to the teacher.
"I wish they had not found it so soon," thought she.
But being a wise teacher, she answered enthusiastically,
"Yes, here he is on the curtain."

"Oh!" and "ah!" breathed the children as they looked
long and wonderingly at the moth, being careful not to
touch him for the teacher suggested this would hurt him.
From previous conversations they knew how the cocoon
had come to be. So the teacher needed only to say,
"When the moth was ready, God made him know how to
come out."

Fred's eyes measured the small hole and the cramped
quarters of the cocoon. He glanced at the lovely brown
moth and in the most reverent tones one could imagine,
said, "Gee, ain't God a brick!" This was the highest
praise he knew. His shining face gave evidence of his
adoring worship.

> Oh, who can make a moth?
> I'm sure I can't, can you?

The teacher softly sang these lines of "Wonder Song"
alone. Then just as softly the children at her knee joined
her in the other lines:

Oh, who can make a moth?
No one but God 'tis true.[1]

There was a moment of silence. Then with bowed heads they thanked God for making beautiful moths come from cocoons.

PLANNING IN ADVANCE

The teacher in the preceding life situation planned for worship. Early in the fall she had begun looking for cocoons and encouraging her children to do likewise. At her suggestion they had brought three or four from their homes. She had anticipated the coming of the first moth, the use she would make of it, and what the children's responses would be. Her plans did not work out just as she had expected, but they did result in a rare worship experience.

Teachers cannot know in advance just what situations, materials, and methods will bring about worship experiences. However, they can build on their knowledge of child nature and on responses which they may expect from Beginners and plan for what may lead to worship.

Usually the worship expressions of four- and five-year-olds are joyous. The children sing because they are happy, and for the same reason they often laugh as they sing. Sometimes, however, they may express their feelings in neither song nor words. Instead the teachers' careful plans may reach fulfilment in the look of worshipful wonder in the children's eyes.

It is possible, too, for teachers to plan so carefully for worship experiences that they may be guilty of coloring the responses of the children to fulfil their own desires. They may read genuine worship into results that are lacking in warmth and appreciation. Careful planning is

---

[1] *Songs for the Pre-School Age* (Nashville: Broadman Press, 1926), p. 22.

important, but there is need also for patient and prayerful waiting for the precious moments when the hearts of the children are ready.

PUTTING THE ROOM IN READINESS

To help to insure worship teachers should put the room in readiness before Sunday. Since the children are susceptible to order and beauty in their surroundings, the teachers should have the room neatly and attractively arranged. The windows should be clear and clean so that the children may see something of God's outdoor world.

MAKING PERSONAL PREPARATION

The attitude and example of the teachers are of more importance than the room in creating an atmosphere in which the children can be led to worship. Each teacher should put herself in readiness for her contact with the children by communion with the Lord before she leaves home. At Sunday school she should continue to seek his presence. She should be ever on the alert for wonderful and beautiful things which she can help the children to see and feel and for which she can lead them to be thankful. This reality of God in the teacher's experience will be sensed by the children and will mean much in leading them into real experiences of worship.

DEVELOPING AN AWARENESS OF GOD

Parents should not confine recognition of God's thoughtfulness in all beautiful things, his love, care, and every home comfort to a few moments at bedtime. They should help their children to feel God's presence in the midst of every happiness. Neither should teachers be satisfied when, at a special time during the session, the children sing, repeat prayer verses and take part in the offering. They should help the children to feel God's presence in all the happy experiences of the Sunday school hour.

DIRECTING CONVERSATION

Often teachers can so direct conversation that the children will become aware of God's presence as they recall good times at home or consider his love and care for all his creatures.

Frequently the questions children ask give the teachers opportunities to speak in an informal way of God's presence. After they had talked together about the church as God's house, a child asked her teacher, "Is God here now in his house?" "Yes," answered the teacher quite naturally, "we cannot see him, of course, but when we get quiet and still and think about his goodness to us we feel his presence."

Thus the way was opened to speak of different evidences of God's presence, such as the sunshine that made soft shadows on the wall, the cool breezes that came in through the windows, and the lovely promises in God's Book.

TELLING STORIES

While most stories suggest desired conduct, give information, or widen experiences, there are some which have none of these missions. If they are told well, in the proper atmosphere and setting, they lead to wonder and to worship. The Christmas stories, the story of Jesus and the children, and the story of the flight into Egypt are often followed by feelings of nearness to God.

SHOWING PICTURES

The use of a picture which shows an individual or a group of people singing may cause the children to desire a similar experience. In like manner the worshipful attitude of the child in the *Infant Samuel* and the people in *The Angelus* may influence them to want to speak to God in prayer. Through their imagination the children enter into the experiences of the pictured people who feel the presence of God.

A picture of Jesus healing or helping invites the children to draw near to see and to touch, and when one child softly says, "I love him," there is usually a chorus of "I love him, too."

In one Beginner department as Christmastime approaches, the teachers place on a low easel a beautiful framed copy of the nativity scene and use a soft artificial light from below in such a way that it seems to emanate from the manger. This always creates an atmosphere in which it is easy to keep Jesus at the center of the children's worship.

READING BIBLE VERSES

Through reading verses from the Bible, which the children are learning to recognize as God's Book, the teachers may help them to feel that God is speaking to them. They sense his presence as they listen to such verses as: "Children, obey your parents," "Love one another," "He hath made every thing beautiful in his time," "The Lord is good to all."

Assurances such as: "The Lord is my helper," "He careth for you," and "Thou art near, O Lord," help the children to feel that God is near enough to hear them when they speak to him in prayer or praise even though they cannot hear him answer.

CONTRIBUTING TO QUIET WONDER

There are times when communion with God is so real that one does not need words. Even little children can sense God's nearness and love and enjoy this companionship of which one need not speak. Finding her small daughter sitting quietly in the sunshine, a mother asked, "What are you doing, darling?" The soft answer came, "I'm just sitting out here with God." It was easy for the mother to believe that God's presence was very real to the child.

There is a sense of worshipful companionship that comes while one is working with God. The cherishing care of children smaller than themselves and of young animals or of working out a plan to bring happiness to others helps little children to worship in this way once they are taught to do so.

USING INSTRUMENTAL MUSIC

Listening to worshipful music may in itself be a worship experience. An alert pianist watches for opportunities to play a beautiful hymn or such an instrumental selection as that from Handel's "Largo," found in *Songs We Sing,* to arouse feelings of wonder and awe.

A group of Beginners had finished decorating their Christmas tree with the pretty things they had made for their mothers and daddies and with small tarletan stockings of money they had brought for the children at the orphanage. A teacher turned on the tree lights. The children stood looking at the tree, some with hands clasped behind them. The pianist began to play softly "Silent Night, Holy Night," the quiet music she had used for the December Sundays. Not a word was said, yet it was not wishful thinking that made the teacher feel that every child was worshiping as he listened. When the music ceased, one child said, "Read us, 'And there were shepherds.'" Because this Bible passage had been read to the children several times during the Sundays before Christmas, it was natural for the child to associate it with the music.

CONSIDERING GIFTS OF NATURE

The seasons bring many opportunities for inspiring awe through the use of God's beautiful out-of-door gifts. Autumn leaves, winter berries, budding branches, peach blossoms, and cut flowers brought into the room, speak to the children of God's goodness and power. Experiences with the rain, snow, wind, or sunshine may lead to joy and appreciation which find expression in talking to God. More often, however, they lead to quiet wonder.

EXPRESSING WORSHIP IN SONG

Singing and melody making have come down through the years as happy means of giving expression to the lifting of hearts toward God. Group singing characterizes the public worship of old and young. As little children thus express their joy or thanksgiving, something in the response of the group adds meaning to the worship of each individual.

CHOOSING FAMILIAR SONGS

Beginners cannot find worship expression in songs with which they are unfamiliar. For this reason, it is important that the teachers in planning for worship or in taking advantage of situations that arise unexpectedly shall select songs that have been used over and over with other experiences.

Not all the songs that are meaningful in worship experiences are songs of praise. Some of them are prayer songs and should be so used. There are also songs which help the children to express their feelings of worshipful appreciation, such as "Wonder Song," from *Songs for the Pre-School Age.* "I Love You," from *Songs We Sing,* is a good example of a musical expression of a child's adoring love for the baby Jesus.

SINGING ORIGINAL SONGS

Original songs of praise and prayer should be treasured as choice expressions of children's worship in song. One child, when he had heard of David's singing songs to God, sang to a tune of his own making the Bible verse used most frequently that day, "O give thanks unto the Lord; for he is good." The tune, caught by the pianist and teachers, was used again and again on that and other Sundays.

LEADING TO WORSHIPFUL PRAYER

The children's experiences at home and Sunday school should give them opportunities to express their love for God and to thank him for definite joys and specific good gifts. Yet adoration and thanksgiving are not all that Beginners' prayers should contain. Even at this early age the children can feel the need of God's help in everyday situations and under wise guidance supplication may have a place in their prayers.

If the children have been properly guided and have something real for which to ask, it will be natural for them to ask God's help. A number of children in one Beginner group were planning to enter kindergarten, and the matter of their safety in crossing streets was of deep concern to their teacher. She told stories which emphasized the necessity of care in watching traffic lights and used the following song:

> Stop, look, listen,
>   Before you cross the street!
> Use your eyes, use your ears,
>   And then, use your feet![2]

[2]*Song and Play for Children* (Boston: Pilgrim Press, 1925), p. 107. Used by permission of Milton Bradley Company.

She stressed the thought that God would help them use their eyes and ears and feet if they would ask him to do so.

Later, one mother reported that her little son was very quiet while they waited for the traffic light to change on their way to kindergarten the first morning. When they had safely crossed the street, he said, "I asked God to help me use my ears and eyes and feet, and he did." And who can say that God did not answer this prayer of supplication?

It is easy to help children to understand that God knows best, and that it is for this reason he sometimes says no to a request even as parents do. This leads to a beginning of submission in their prayers and becomes a safeguard to their faith when experiences of seemingly unanswered petitions come to them even as they come to all.

There is rarely, if ever, an occasion when a Beginner at Sunday school should confess his personal wrongdoing. Such a prayer is sometimes a part of his home experience but it should remain a private matter which has no place in his Sunday school experiences.

ENCOURAGING SPONTANEOUS PRAYER

Children should be helped to talk often to God in their own words but the words should always be an expression of real feeling. With this readiness taken into account, the teacher may say occasionally: "We have had a happy time together this morning and I want to thank God for something special. It may be that each of you also has something special for which you would like to thank him." As heads are bowed, she may say very naturally: "Dear God, thank you for the roses Betty brought." After a brief pause, one of the teachers may say: "Dear God, thank you for the green trees." Both of these prayers may be repeated by the children and then several of the children may, in turn, express their thanks in their own words.

Another way to help bring about the same result is to use a song like the following as a litany:

> We thank you, God,
> We thank you, God,
> For ....
> We thank you, God.[3]

The words may be spoken quietly instead of sung and may include any good gift the children mention. Birds that sing, flowers that bloom, bright sunshine, food to eat, clothes to wear, and many others may be fitted to the rhythm.

TRAINING IN PRAYER EXPRESSION

The teacher may help the children in their prayer expression by making the prayer in very simple words and letting the children repeat it sentence by sentence. Or she may make the prayer and let the children say "Amen" at the conclusion. In either instance she should anticipate the feelings of the children or ask them to make suggestions and be very specific. Generalities enter into adults' prayers but children thank God for "good oatmeal," for "my white kitten," for "my mother and daddy." One group prayer, at a child's request, included a thank-you for "Joan's grandmother who is *her mother*."

While other prayers should be used more often at home and Sunday school, there is a definite value in the use of well-chosen form prayers. Many parents and teachers have long since discarded the time-honored form which suggests that a child may die before he wakes. They use instead forms that encourage feelings of security and

[3] *Songs We Sing* (Nashville: Broadman Press, 1939), p. 8.

that express what the children would like to say in more beautiful words than they have at their command.

Beautiful form prayers particularly help children to learn the language of prayer. The rhythm of a form or poem-prayer is very attractive to them and herein lies a danger against which teachers should guard. If the same prayer is used too frequently, the rhythm rather than the thought it expresses may become uppermost in the children's experience.

GUIDING IN WORSHIPFUL GIVING

The gifts of money which the children bring to God's house are usually spoken of as "love gifts," but they are love gifts only when they are intelligently and willingly given and are received in a spirit of worship by the teachers. A common problem is the lack of understanding about what is done with them. It is not unusual for children to get the idea that their teachers use the money for pretty clothes or that in some mysterious way the money is actually sent up to God.

Such erroneous ideas may be avoided and the bringing of gifts made a worshipful experience for the children if the teachers are careful to explain Sunday after Sunday that in bringing their gifts they show their love for God and help to carry on his work. Even Beginners can understand that money is needed to keep up repairs on the church building, to buy coal to keep it warm, and to pay the janitor for keeping it clean. They can understand also that money is needed to pay for the lovely lesson materials and to help send the story of Jesus to other children far and near. Before they do understand, however, they need to be told many times. Before they can give joyously, they must feel a desire to give and also find satisfaction in so doing.

Giving is often more meaningful to children and becomes a more satisfying experience if it takes the form of sharing. Teachers should so guide them that they will learn early to share the things that make others happy —things that they can make and their personal treasures as well as money.

It was an experience in real giving when a group of Beginners had a linen shower for an orphanage near their church which had lost a dormitory wing by fire. It was also real giving when the same group as a climax to a unit of lessons about God's house bought their pastor a potted plant as a love gift, and slipped in to place it in the big church before time for the morning worship service.

Simple gifts can be made by four- and five-year-olds to help make people happier or to show their love for them. The sharing of a child's home treasures, such as toys, shells, or picture books with his friends at Sunday school, is a beautiful form of giving. Sharing things he cannot touch or see, such as well-loved songs and stories, also may become a part of his giving.

At some time during the session all the gifts should be dedicated. The money which was placed in receptacles as the children arrived, the handwork that was done to make someone happy, and even the flowers which were brought to make God's house beautiful should all be talked about informally, and God's blessing asked upon them. Such a service, which may include a Bible verse, a song, or a prayer, often makes the difference between giving in a mechanical way and giving as an act of worship.

Regardless of whether the children worship silently or express it in song, prayer, or giving, every experience is precious in the sight of the Lord. It is also precious in the lives of the children, for it makes a deposit nothing can take away.

CHAPTER OUTLINE

CHAPTER VII

MAKING AND USING PROGRAM PLANS

The Sunday morning session should be a series of happy experiences for the children and should lead to desirable outcomes. To this end plans must be carefully made and skilfully used.

MAKING PROGRAM PLANS

Responsibility for making the plans rests largely upon the superintendent-teacher, but she will find it advantageous to make them with the other workers of the department. If it is not possible for the workers to plan together, they should make individual preparation, compare notes, and agree upon definite plans for every session. This is necessary to co-operative effort in using the plans.

STUDYING THE LESSON

Naturally the making of plans should begin with a study of the lesson chosen for the day. "Open thou mine eyes, that I may behold wondrous things out of thy law," the prayer of the psalmist of old, should continually be in the hearts of the teachers as they read and reread the Scripture passage upon which the lesson is based. In connection with the lessons offered by the Baptist Sunday School Board, the *Teacher's Book* carries a printed Scripture passage and references for additional readings to enrich the teacher's background. It also carries a helpful treatment of the lesson, including suggested activities for the entire session. Teachers should become thoroughly familiar with all these helps and should read carefully the leaflet for the children.

See lesson in relation to the unit.—Since the lessons are grouped in units of learning, teachers should always see

the lesson in relation to the unit of which it is a part.
For instance, there are five lessons in a unit, "Learning
About God." Each lesson is designed to make a specific contribution to the desired outcome of the unit
which is:

To give little children a growing conception of
God as the loving Heavenly Father who is always
near to help them; to lead them to think of him as
making the world and other things for them to enjoy.

Thus, for these five Sundays, the teachers should not
only consider the teaching possibilities of the individual
lesson but also seek so to use the material that each lesson will accomplish its purpose as a part of the unit.

Some of the Bible stories which children love best may
be used in connection with units that have different
teaching objectives. As an illustration, the story of
the coming of the baby Jesus may be used in connection
with a unit the purpose of which is to help the children
develop a love for Bible stories. It may be a part of
a unit designed to lead the children to an appreciation
of their homes and their mothers. It may also be included in a unit of lessons the purpose of which is to
make Jesus the center of the children's thinking at
Christmastime, stressing God's best Gift. The teachers
should always plan to use the story in accordance with
the teaching emphasis of the unit.

Consider seasonal or special needs.—Beginners are
particularly interested in what is going on in the world
about them, and the changing seasons bring many teaching opportunities. Following the example of Jesus,
teachers should be on the alert to take advantage of any
teaching opportunity which the world of nature offers
if it comes within the realm of the children's experiences.

Suggestions for using seasonal opportunities are given regularly in the *Beginner Teacher*, but teachers must remember that this book is prepared for use in many localities and that seasons and conditions vary. Children in Kentucky, for instance, see robins building nests in the spring, but children in Alabama think of robins as "flocks of birds that spend the winter with us," as only a few remain to build nests.

There are times, too, when co-operation in the general plans of a local church or the special need of an individual or a group of children requires special plans for one or more sessions. In one church when the parents and older friends of the children were engaged in a church loyalty campaign, the Beginner teachers co-operated by including in their plans special efforts to deepen the children's appreciation of God's house and all that goes on there.

On another occasion a mother was distressed because her five-year-old son was developing an attitude of cruelty toward animals. She appealed to the Beginner teachers who gladly made a place in their teaching plans for stories and experiences to meet this definite need. Following the introduction of a basket of puppies, which the children were shown how to handle without hurting, the child asked for a dog of his own. Under the guidance of the mother and encouraged by the teacher's interest and tactful suggestions from time to time, the boy learned to care for his pet as well as any child of his age could have been expected to do.

Decide what the lesson ought to accomplish.—The purpose of the lesson becomes the purpose of the session, and unless seasonal or special needs make adjustments necessary, teachers may well follow the suggestions offered in the *Teacher's Book.* In so doing they should make this purpose their own and keep it ever in mind as they plan for the session and as they guide the activities on Sunday morning.

LISTING TEACHING MATERIALS

Materials for which the teachers think they will probably find use during the session should be carefully listed. The list should include pictures, play equipment, gifts of nature, Bible verses, songs, and other materials which they may arrange in centers of interest or use in various ways. All materials should point to the purpose of the session.

PLANNING POSSIBLE ACTIVITIES

There are some types of activities, of course, in which the children may profitably engage every Sunday. Singing, conversing, and listening to stories should have a place in the plans for every session. It is not practicable or desirable, however, to include in the plans for any one session all the types of activity that may be used effectively. The activities should be selected in accordance with the appeal they make to the children's interests, the relation they have to the teaching emphasis for the day, and their values in giving balance to the procedure.

Consider interest appeal.—Since Beginners enjoy some activities more than others, their enjoyment should be a matter for consideration when choices are being made. Teachers should not forget that children respond as individuals. Activities that are interesting and helpful to some children may not be equally interesting and helpful to others. Examining pictures means more to some children than it does to others. Listening to worshipful music helps some children to feel God's presence near, while hearing a story about his love makes others more conscious of his nearness. There should be enough variety in the activities to care for the children's individual interests.

Relate to teaching emphasis.—Every activity which is planned for a session should relate to the teaching emphasis. To illustrate, informal, dramatic, or representative play easily relates to a teaching emphasis of sharing or helping. Singing songs about helping or sharing, examining pictures of people sharing or helping, and selecting pictures to share with children in another Sunday school also relate definitely to the emphasis.

If the purpose of the session is to deepen appreciation of God's love and care, songs of love and praise may be used. Other related activities may be handling and talking about God's gifts through nature, looking at pictures of children enjoying his gift of water, and playing in the sunshine he provides. Making pictures of "his good gifts to me" and taking a walk through an imaginary park and talking about the trees and flowers are also activities that definitely relate to the teaching emphasis.

Obviously, the suggested activities do not include all that relate to the teaching emphasis in either of the examples here given.

Always the teacher should be mindful that children need repetition and a feeling of security built upon familiar surroundings and activities, but they also need enough of the new to catch their interest and keep learning an ongoing process.

Avoid monotony and overstimulation.—Another matter to bear in mind in choosing the activities is that the session should be neither monotonous nor overstimulating. If the plans provide for the children to be seated most of the time during the early part of the hour, making gifts or doing other types of handwork, a stimulating dramatization is in order later. Often the singing of a song effectively follows listening to a story, and soft music is appropriate after active representative play.

As previously suggested, children need to learn the language of prayer, and plans should frequently include rote prayers. They need also to voice the love and thankfulness that fill their hearts, and plans should provide opportunities for spontaneous expression. They need the feeling of security which accompanies the singing of a song like "God Takes Care of Me," but they also need the stimulation of such a song as "Friendly Children," both of which are found in *Songs We Sing*.

Both representative play and story dramatization are valuable activities but they should not be used too frequently. If the plans provide for the children to play "sweeping and dusting" every time the teaching emphasis for the day is helping, or to play out the story every time one lends itself to dramatization, these happy forms will tend to lose their sparkle and freshness.

The children's ability to sing and the joy they find in singing do not justify giving the major portion of every session to this activity. Neither does the fact that drawing appeals to the children's interest and keeps them quiet give sufficient reason for using this activity every Sunday. Singing songs must not degenerate into a time filler and drawing must not become mere busy-ness.

OUTLINING A TENTATIVE PROGRAM

So unpredictable are little children that the word "tentative" is used advisedly. Careful planning, however, makes it possible for the teachers to accomplish their purpose for the day even though they do not follow the procedure as outlined.

Recognize basic principles.—The characteristics of the children and the ways in which they learn make informality and flexibility essential. The informal way is the natural and therefore the happy way for them. There are some things, of course, which they need to do over and over in the same way to build that foundation of the familiar which is necessary to a feeling of security. For example, providing a regular place to hang their outdoor clothing and placing the offering basket in the same place Sunday after Sunday help the children to feel sure about the proper things to do on arrival. "We hang up our wraps" and "We put our love gifts in the basket" become simple rules which they find satisfaction in obeying. "We put up our toys when Miss M......... plays 'A Helper I Will Be,'" may also become a simple and happy rule if the pianist uses this song regularly as a signal for them to assemble in a large group.

At all times, however, an atmosphere of freedom and informality should invite the children to move about and to engage in activities that appeal especially to their interests. Teachers should help them to feel that the pictures are for them to examine and enjoy, the blocks are for them to play with if they so desire, and other materials are for them to use and share.

The children need not always sit in a circle for conversation and stories even when they assemble in one group. They may sit on a rug, in chairs drawn close about the superintendent-teacher's knee, or stand looking out of the window when these are the natural things to do.

To guard against this informality being confused with license, the word "orderly" is often used in connection with it. Skilful guidance on the part of the teachers should preclude any disorder.

Flexibility in program plans anticipates interruptions and changes. The plans may provide for the singing of one song but they will yield readily to another if it is the children's desire or if an unexpected situation makes it more appropriate. Flexibility anticipates questions and other contributions from the children. It allows for new or special features to give place to a recalled story or the sharing of experiences that have been shared before without diverting the program from its original purpose. It is often indicated in program outlines by the use of the words "if," "or," and "provided."

Provide for essential elements.—Fellowship, learning, and worship are three elements which plans for every session should provide. Experiences in fellowship include the exchange of greetings, participation in the joy of one another's birthdays, rejoicing together over the coming of baby brothers and sisters, and being sorry when sorrow or misfortune comes to a member of the group. They include also a sense of unity in working, playing, and singing together and participating in service or courtesy enterprises for friends near and far.

Previous considerations of learning and worship experiences have shown how vital they are to every worth-while program. The children do not enjoy fellowship at one time, learn at another, and worship at another. These experiences are closely related and often intermingled. The joy of being with friends, which is fellowship, enriches the singing of praise to God, which is worship. When the children are working and playing together, they are also learning to live together happily. Again, they may be examining a birds' nest. As their little fists snuggle down where baby birds have slept warmly and safely, they learn about the birds' God-given skill, and worshipful wonder over God's plans for the lives of birds may begin somewhere during the learning experience—just where no one can tell.

Teachers cannot plan these elements separately and set definite times for each in the program plans, but they should plan for the entire session to be an interwoven experience of fellowship, learning, and worship.

Follow a natural order.—The questions What shall we plan to do first? and What shall we plan to do next? may be answered with other questions, What would the children like to do first? and What would naturally follow? With these questions to guide them and with the teaching objectives, the materials, and possible activities in mind, the teachers can plan what they think will be a natural, orderly procedure to a desired end.

When making an outline the teachers will find it helpful to state where the Scripture lesson is to be found, to mention the title of the lesson and the lesson unit, and to write the purpose of the lesson.

The following outline is suggestive of a procedure that might be planned for one Sunday morning:

SMALL GROUP

Exchanging friendly greetings

Giving needed help for the disposal of hats and wraps

Participation in activity at a center of interest

LARGE GROUP

Singing a familiar greeting song

Sharing experiences and showing work done in small groups

Giving recognition to:

Visitors and new members

Members who have been absent

Members who have had a birthday

Singing songs of praise

Recalling Bible verses through the use of:
    Pictures
    Questions
    "Playlike" Bibles
    Familiar story incidents
Speaking to God in prayer
Bringing the love gifts:
    Singing about them
    Using Bible verses
    Talking to God about them
Providing rest and relaxation through such activities
as:
    Taking a picture walk
    Flying like birds
    Skipping to rhythm
Singing a special song related to the teaching emphasis
Telling the Bible story
Showing a large teaching picture
Examining the leaflets with the children

Conversation is not mentioned in the outline because it is not something separate. It is the woof which runs in and out of the warp of many different threads of experiences and binds them into a beautiful whole. So important is it that one may say the session is a conversation in which songs, prayers, purposive handwork, and play are introduced. Even stories to which the children listen may be considered contributions to the conversation. Informal play is made more valuable because it invites the children to talk with one another and with the teachers. The success of dramatic play is dependent on conversation to initiate and get ready for it.

As the children arrive they are checked by the department secretary. They will go to the center of interest of their choice and there engage in an activity from twenty to thirty minutes.

(There may be times when it is desirable for all the children to engage in an activity such as making gifts for parents. For this the superintendent may reserve ten or fifteen minutes at the close of the large group in which the children may work together.)

A simple melody may be played for the children to put away their materials and come to the large group.

The large group activities will occupy the remainder of the time left from the small groups. The time in the small group will vary according to the activities going on in the small groups.

The teachers guide the activities in the small group while the superintendent guides the activities in the large group.

Each teacher will sit in or near the large group and participate in the activities with the children.

The recognition of visitors, new members, and returned absentees should be very simple. Beginners consider it quite an honor to stand before the group while a bright song is sung accompanied by the waving of hands.

The bringing of a birthday offering of a penny for each year is a long-established custom in many Sunday schools. A four- or five-year-old appreciates the privilege of choosing a friend to hold the receptacle while he deposits the pennies and other members of the group count them. A song and prayer may follow. In some departments it is customary to give the child a simple favor. The lighting of candles is discouraged at Sunday school for accidents have happened and may happen again.

USING PROGRAM PLANS

There is always a feeling of adventure in connection with a Sunday session with Beginners. Teachers can never know what will happen to their carefully made plans. With calmness and confidence born of thorough preparation they should work together, not to carry out the plans as made but so to use them that they will accomplish the most good to the children.

ADJUSTING TO MEET NEEDS

Sometimes teachers are justified in changing their purpose to meet needs that arise. Usually, however, necessary changes are confined to the order or items of procedure.

The Bible story, as an example, may be planned to come near the close of the session and climax the program, as it does in the suggestive outline. Or plans may provide for it to come early in the session and so give opportunity for expression through the features that follow. In either case, if the opportune moment for telling the story should come at another time, it should be recognized and used.

Similar changes may be necessary in connection with other activities. Centers of interest which the teachers have planned may fail in their appeal as children gather about centers they set up for themselves. The songs which the teachers have selected may give place to others which are requested by the group or to one song which the children choose to sing in connection with various experiences.

USING UNEXPECTED OPPORTUNITIES

Unexpected situations may hinder or help, depending upon the ability of the teachers to recognize the teaching opportunities the new situations offer, and their skill in using them. One morning the children in a department promptly responded to the familiar signal and skipped as they assembled in the large group. In some way a little boy tripped and fell, striking his head against the piano. Of course, there was a scream and as the super-intendent-teacher drew him close to her, the children gathered about them and all tried to talk at the same time. The child who had fallen was more scared than hurt and soon forgot himself as the others told about accidents and sickness which had brought doctors into their homes. The superintendent-teacher watched for her opportunity and as part of her contribution to the conversation told the story of the father who went to Jesus for help when his son was ill, which happened to be the Bible story for the day. The children listened with keen interest and eagerly examined the lesson picture. Then they quietly took their places in the circle. The superintendent-teacher quickly made the necessary changes in the plans and led them to sing, pray, and engage in other activities. There was no break in the continuity of thought. Everything moved on as smoothly as if the original plans were being carried out.

FOLLOWING THE CHILDREN'S LEAD

Some of the children's contributions need only to be received courteously and passed over, for they have no relation to the discussion at hand and do not give promise of usefulness in other ways. There are others, however, which are very valuable. These reveal present interests to which teachers may appeal and suggest needs which the plans can be adjusted to meet. It is possible for the children to lead entirely away from the plans for the day but usually the teachers have only to follow the lead a short way and come back to the original plans and purposes with the full co-operation of the children.

EVALUATING THE SESSION

Evaluation has come to be an everyday word with those who would achieve. Beginner teachers who would constantly improve their work will therefore do well to practice looking back and evaluating the session. The following questions may be used helpfully in this connection:

1. Did we, as teachers, find the session a satisfying experience? If not, why?

2. Were our plans well-made? What weak points were evident?

3. Did we properly magnify the Bible and find occasions for using familiar verses when and where they had meaning for the children?

4. Did we introduce too much new material?

5. Was there participation on the part of each child? What activities elicited the most general participation?

6. Were the children unhurried, or were we guilty of rushing them from one activity to another?

7. Did we provide enough variety to make the session interesting? Was it overstimulating?

8. Was there an atmosphere in which it was easy for the children to work and play together?

9. Did we succeed in getting worth-while responses?

10. Were there evidences that the activities actually resulted in desirable learning experiences?

11. Were there any unexpected situations offering opportunity for actual practice in needed learnings? Did we recognize and use the situations?

12. Did we answer the children's questions thoughtfully or did we evade them?

13. Did we help the children to worship? Was their giving a worship experience?

14. Did the songs we chose fulfil their mission? Did the children enter into the singing with joy and enthusiasm?

15. Can we profit by any of today's experiences in making another session more helpful?

It is important that such an evaluation be made as soon as possible after a session. While experiences are still fresh in the minds of the teachers, they may rejoice together over all that went well and at the same time face with frankness any disappointments and unused opportunities. Only so can they best profit from their mistakes and become increasingly skilful in making and using program plans.

CHAPTER OUTLINE

Co-operating in the General Assembly

Making Department Periods Helpful
Pray Together for Help and Guidance
Introduce Special Features
Make and Discuss Reports
Talk Over Specific Problems
Make Departmental Plans
Plan the Sunday Session
Study to Improve Teaching
Set up Administrative Objectives
Adopt the Standard of Excellence

Holding Special Department Conferences
Select a Suitable Place and Time
Prepare Worth-while Programs

CHAPTER VIII

PLANNING TOGETHER IN THE WEEKLY OFFICERS AND TEACHERS' MEETING

Beginner teachers who take their task seriously recognize their need for meeting regularly in the interest of their department. They recognize also that the department is not a separate organization but part of a larger unit, the Sunday school. Its interests are closely tied up with those of the school as a whole. If they are to do their best for the children, they must help to set up the school's aims and over-all plans and relate themselves properly to its general activities. This calls for consultation and co-operative planning with the general officers and the officers and teachers of the other departments. Only so can they be "labourers together" in the work to which God has called them. They find their opportunity for such department and general planning in the weekly officers and teachers' meeting.

The meeting is held under the leadership of the pastor and the general superintendent. Usually it is scheduled to take place on Wednesday evening, but any more convenient time may be chosen. It is held at the church and it is often preceded by a supper. Such a custom not only contributes to the convenience of many workers but also helps the workers in the various departments to know and to love one another, thus making it easy for them to work together happily.

The program for the meeting provides for a general assembly of the workers and a period of thirty to forty-five minutes when they meet in separate groups for the consideration of the work in their particular departments.

CO-OPERATING IN THE GENERAL ASSEMBLY

The Sunday school superintendent usually presides over the general period. After a brief season of worship and the making of necessary announcements, he presents for discussion matters which are of interest to all departments.

From time to time questions relating to the maintaining of proper organization and the adjusting of space and equipment to meet changing needs are discussed. Goals are set and plans are made for such special occasions as training schools, enlargement campaigns, and the observance of denominational days.

At one meeting each month the superintendent asks for reports from the various departments. Beginner teachers have a responsibility in all these activities. They should be present to take part in the discussions and the planning and should faithfully and honestly report both the successes and the problems of their department.

Frequently the pastor brings a word of greeting—sometimes to encourage and strengthen and again to challenge to greater effort. Because earnest teachers draw so deeply from themselves and give out so continuously, they need constant spiritual refreshment. Beginner teachers especially need the stimulus of spiritual contact with more mature minds than those of their children. These needs should give them a vital interest in their pastor's messages.

MAKING DEPARTMENT PERIODS HELPFUL

The superintendent-teacher is responsible for planning and conducting the department period, but she should not be expected to do all the work. All the teachers should have a part in making the period interesting and helpful. The brevity of the time at their disposal should lead them to make careful plans and carry them out promptly and effectively.

PRAY TOGETHER FOR HELP AND GUIDANCE

Even though there is a period of devotion in the general assembly, Beginner teachers, when they meet in the interest of their particular work, should take time to meditate on God's Word. They need to pray for the help and guidance of the Holy Spirit in making plans and carrying them to completion. The superintendent-teacher may ask different co-workers to lead this brief devotion. She should make such requests well in advance in order that they may make real preparation for the few minutes which are to set the tone of the entire period.

INTRODUCE SPECIAL FEATURES

There is no better way to add variety and interest to the meetings than to introduce an occasional special feature. The possibilities here are endless. A worker from another Sunday school may tell how her department solved some problem the group faces. The librarian may review a new book from the church library. Someone may read an inspirational poem, tell a story, or read an excerpt from the *Beginner Teacher*, *The Sunday School Builder*, or some other magazine which has a particular interest for the group.

Occasionally the special feature may be a bit of fun or an opportunity for group fellowship. Because people work together better when they are bound by the ties of friendship as well as common interests, such friendship devices as are popular in Adult classes may be effective. For example, each teacher may draw the name of a friend to whom she may send little anonymous gifts or manifest her friendliness in some other way until a specified time, when all names will be divulged.   Such special features should never require more than five minutes.

MAKE AND DISCUSS REPORTS

Records play a very important part in the success of the work of the department, and the secretary should be ready at each meeting to make a brief but helpful report, comparing the attendance of the last Sunday with that of the previous Sunday and with the corresponding Sunday of the preceding year.   In their discussion of the report, the teachers should mention by name those who were absent the last Sunday and consider such questions as: Was the absence caused by illness?   Was it due to a week-end trip, a transportation problem, or indifference on the part of the child or his parents?   What was done about it?   What more can be done to prevent a recurrence?

Teachers should carefully check on both absentees and tardy pupils in the advance of the meeting.   They should be prepared to talk about these members of their groups in such a way that they will not be merely names on cards to the other teachers but living children who have been entrusted to the care of the department for two brief but important years.

In many departments both the superintendent-teacher and the teachers keep loose-leaf notebooks, allowing two or more pages for the record of each child in the department or group.   The following form is suggestive:

'Pupil's name ....
Address .... Phone ....
Age...... Date of birth......... Date enrolled.......
Parent's name ....
Father a church member...... Where?..............
Mother a church member...... Where?..............

Mother employed?........... Where?...............
Father's occupation.....................................
Did the child attend Nursery School?.................
Is the child attending Kindergarten?.................
Where? ....
What is the attitude of the parents toward the child?
....
Do the parents play with the child?...............
Do the parents have a quiet time with the child?......
....
Do the parents take walks with the child?..........
Do the parents read to the child?...................
Do the parents tell stories to the child?...............
Does the child play alone?........ With others?......
What ages? ....
Are there other members of the family?...............
Name and ages ....
....
Is the home above average, average, below average, eco-
nomically?.................. socially?............
educationally? ....
What are the needs of the child?...................
....
....
Are there specific problems?.........If so check them:
fear........ shyness...... insecurity...... selfish-
ness....... aggressiveness....... (You may have to
add others to this list) ....
....
What are some of the experiences of the child?........
....
As you observe the child from Sunday to Sunday jot
down anything which you consider worth while in his
development ....
....

Such a study will not only help the teachers in choosing methods and materials for teaching the children but will also enable them to check regularly and accurately on each child's progress. For instance, on entering the department Johnny Doe's disposition may be checked as *sullen and selfish*. If the teachers not only recognize his need but also endeavor to meet it, they may in a few weeks be able to record that he is beginning to be *more cheerful* and to enjoy *sharing with others*. On the other hand, they may find a lack of improvement and be challenged to a greater effort in the child's behalf.

In like manner, the study may make note of important changes in the child's home life. His parents may be recorded as *indifferent* but later, as a result of the department's efforts, the record may be changed to *co-operative*. They may be listed as *unaffiliated Baptists* until the teacher through interest in the child, visits in the home, invitations to the church service, and tactful conversation about the program of the church, helps them to realize the importance of taking their places in its life and work. Along with the joy she will find in welcoming them into the church fellowship will come the privilege of changing the record in her book.

TALK OVER SPECIFIC PROBLEMS

Frequently the teachers have specific problems for which they must find solutions. Their equipment may be inadequate. There may be an obstreperous child in the group or a critical parent who makes trouble. Tardiness, irregular attendance, or a tendency on the part of the teachers to talk among themselves during the session may be hindering the work. There is no better time or place than in this weekly meeting to face the problem squarely, talk it over frankly and impersonally, and endeavor to arrive at a solution.

Make Departmental Plans

Occasionally the teachers need to arrange a party or picnic for the children or a meeting for mothers. They should always choose a day which does not conflict with other church activities and make very definite plans for the occasion. At different seasons they must make plans for Thanksgiving, Christmas, Mother's Day, and other special occasions, being careful to emphasize their spiritual significance by providing such helps as pictures, songs, stories, and the necessary materials for gift making and other desired manual activities.

Plan the Sunday Session

Emphasis has already been given to the importance of teachers co-operating in planning for Sunday morning. Before they make any plans it is important also for them to check on the previous Sunday's session and consider where their plans worked and where more effective teaching resulted from following leads of the children. They should use the suggestions for evaluating a session and making plans which chapter 7 offers.

Study to Improve Teaching

There is no more important administrative duty connected with the work of the department than helping the teachers to improve their knowledge of the Bible, the children, and Beginner teaching methods. Much of this must necessarily be done at times other than during the regular weekly meetings. Nevertheless a place on every program should be dedicated to this objective.

For example, the devotional moments and an occasional Bible quiz may stimulate interest in and a study of the Bible. Sometimes there may be a quiz on Bible facts. Again there may be a "That reminds me" exercise in which one person suggests something that a Bible character did, said, or taught, and other members respond with something that another Bible character did, said, or taught, of which the first suggestions reminds them. There may be a quick recall of verses on some special theme or of persons who had experiences in common. Occasionally there may be time for the interpretation of a psalm, a teaching from one of the Testaments, or an Adult Sunday school lesson that holds special interest for the group.

Similarly, the teachers should seize every opportunity to learn more about Beginner children and to improve their skill in teaching them.

Books on child study offer valuable suggestions which may become the basis for discussion at many meetings. Articles on special needs and characteristics of Beginners, such as those which frequently appear in *The Sunday School Builder*, may be helpfully considered and discussed.

SET UP ADMINISTRATIVE OBJECTIVES

It is a good thing for the teachers to stop occasionally, especially at the beginning of a new Sunday school year to consider why they are working with the children. It is also helpful to set out definitely and clearly what they hope to accomplish before the children are promoted to the Primary department.

Because teaching is the primary purpose of the department, as of the school, it will be natural to start with teaching objectives. These are discussed at some length in the companion book, *Guiding the Little Child in the Sunday School*, by Elizabeth McEwen Shields. Therefore, it is not necessary to include them here. However, the teachers should carefully consider them with the following administrative or promotional objectives.

1. To discover, enlist, and develop teachers and officers of childlike spirit and growing Christian personality who love and understand little children.

2. To provide a department room adequate in size and attractively furnished in keeping with the needs of children four and five years of age.

3. To discover and enlist all Beginner possibilities.

4. To help the children feel free and happy and at home in their department room.

5. To provide a well-balanced program of teacher-pupil activity.

6. To provide satisfying experiences in worship, learning of God, working and playing together happily, and doing things for others.

7. To make studied provision for giving ever-increasing usable knowledge of the stories, verses, and teachings of God's Word; for developing Christlike attitudes and giving patterns of and encouraging conduct pleasing to God.

8. To co-operate in every possible way with the parents in the religious teaching of their children, and to enlist their intelligent co-operation and support in the work of the department.

There may be other objectives large and small which should be listed. Teachers will find it helpful to study the needs and opportunities in their own situation and prepare individual lists for comparison and consideration. They will then be in position to decide upon objectives which they can reasonably hope to reach during the two years that each child will spend with them. Not until they set up some such goals can they worthily judge the effectiveness of their work.

ADOPT THE STANDARD OF EXCELLENCE

The Baptist Sunday School Board offers Standards of Excellence for the Sunday school and for departments of the Sunday school. Beginner teachers should not only give wholehearted co-operation in connection with the Standard for the school but should also adopt the Beginner Standard as a guide to increased efficiency in their own department.

Study requirements.—The first step to take in adopting the Beginner Standard is to study its requirements. It does not include everything that the department may do, but it does include those things that are necessary to an adequate program of work. Because these requirements are subject to changes, they are not given here. Teachers can get a free copy of the latest Standard by writing to their state Sunday school secretary or to the Department of Sunday School Work, Baptist Sunday School Board, Nashville 3, Tennessee.

Set a time to reach each point.—A definite time limit will help to co-ordinate the department efforts to attain the Standard. Often a department which lacks only a point or two can with an added impetus soon meet all requirements. Even when there is more work to be done, a suggested time limit will help to determine just how soon each point can be attained and encourage work to that end.

Determine to maintain requirements.—To attain the Standard is a worthy achievement, but it is not enough. To be truly Standard a department must maintain the requirements. In order to do this, the teachers will need frequently to check their work by the Standard and to put forth extra effort in connection with points they find difficulty in maintaining.

Obviously the limited time at their disposal will not permit the teachers to engage in all suggested activities at any meeting. In making choices they should be guided by the urgency of department problems, the immediate appeal of seasonal interests, and the need for co-operation in the general plans of the school.

HOLDING SPECIAL DEPARTMENT CONFERENCES

Plans should never be made to take the place of or to interfere with the weekly officers and teachers' meeting. There are some situations, however, in which no provision is made for such a meeting or for a monthly workers' conference. There are other situations in which the plans for such meetings do not allow sufficient time for the department period to make possible all the activities for which Beginner teachers feel the need. In either case, the solution to the problem may be found in special conferences for Beginner teachers which may be held once a month.

SELECT A SUITABLE PLACE AND TIME

Local conditions should be taken into consideration in deciding upon the place and time of the conferences. A group of teachers who are homemakers may choose to meet in the morning and close at noon with a luncheon. Instead, they may find it more convenient to meet in the afternoon and at the close of the session promote fellowship through a social period during which light refreshments are served. If the group includes schoolteachers or businesswomen, late afternoon or evening conferences may be arranged. These suggestions take it for granted that meetings will be held in the homes of the workers, but they may be held elsewhere if it seems more convenient or desirable.

Regardless of the type and place of meeting, the teachers should decide upon a regular day and hour. This is necessary in order that all may consider it a definite engagement and refrain from making conflicting dates.

PREPARE WORTH-WHILE PROGRAMS

If the meeting is held in lieu of the regular weekly officers and teachers' meeting, the activities suggested for that occasion should naturally be brought over into it, and any features added which may be needed or desired. If it is held in addition to the regular weekly meeting, program plans should include any items for which more time is needed than the department period of the regular meeting affords. For example, this occasion is a more appropriate time to have a guest speaker, to outline a program of work for the year, and to make a study of the Standard of Excellence. The lengthened time also gives larger opportunities for the making of plans in connection with special occasions and the preparation of handwork and other materials needed for a unit of lessons.

Teachers often prepare a yearbook in which the places and dates of meetings and program outlines appear. It serves the double purpose of making more binding obligations in connection with the programs and of helping the teachers to anticipate pleasure and profit in attending the meetings.

The story is told of a preacher who received and accepted an invitation to preach in a small church in a neighboring district. He arrived early, accompanied by his young son and found in the vestibule of the church a collection box. Above the box was a notice to the effect that it was customary for members and friends to place their offering therein as there would be no collection taken during the service. The preacher dropped fifty cents in the box and took a place near the front of the church to await the assembling of the people. At the close of the meeting someone charged with the responsibility told him that it was also customary for the visiting preacher to receive the gifts that had been placed in the box as a token of appreciation of his services. Accordingly, the box was opened, and the preacher was given all it contained—the fifty cents which he had placed there. It was then that the little son, who had been an interested onlooker, remarked, "Father, if you had put more in the box, you would have got more out of it." Even so the interest, the co-operation, and the effort that the individual teacher puts into the weekly officers and teachers' meeting and the special Beginner conferences determine the blessings she receives from them.

CHAPTER OUTLINE

OBSERVING PROMOTION DAY
  Appreciating Its Purpose
  Making It a Happy Occasion

PROMOTING CHRISTIAN HOME WEEK
  Getting Ready for the Observance
  Carrying out the Plans

FAMILY-IN-CHURCH DAY
PROVIDING A VACATION BIBLE SCHOOL
  Recognizing the Importance
  Accepting the Challenge

PARTICIPATING IN A TRAINING PROGRAM
  Studying in Training Schools
  Using Other Means of Growth

CHAPTER IX

CO-OPERATING WITH OTHER DEPARTMENTS

In addition to the weekly officers and teachers' meeting, the Sunday school calendar of activities provides four special opportunities for co-operation between the Beginner and the other departments of the school. Promotion Day, a whole school program, and Home Co-operation Week, a project which may be promoted by the four Elementary departments or by all departments of the school, are scheduled for the fall of the year. The Vacation Bible school, which should be for the Beginner, Primary, Junior, and Intermediate departments, is a late spring or summer activity. Programs of intensive training in which all Sunday school workers and prospective workers are asked to take part are scheduled for October and April.

OBSERVING PROMOTION DAY

The designated date for the observance of Promotion Day is the last Sunday in September. On this occasion the senior group from each department is promoted to a higher department. All Beginner children who are six years old, or who will be six by January 1 or April 1, according to the policy of the school, are promoted to the Primary department. The Beginner department, in turn, receives from the Cradle Roll department all members who are four years old or who will be by the accepted date, regardless of whether or not they have had experience in the Nursery Class.

Appreciating Its Purpose

The annual observance of Promotion Day is necessary to maintain the proper grading of the school. It is an important occasion in the pupils' lives, for it marks the passing of a milestone in their Sunday school experience. It is a time for the giving of recognitions and encouragement and for making new and better plans for the months that lie ahead.

Making It a Happy Occasion

What the occasion means to Beginners depends upon the attitude of the teachers and the care with which they prepare for it. They can make it a time of orderliness and rejoicing or allow it to be one of confusion and tears.

Begin preparations early.—As a first step in preparation for Promotion Day, the superintendent-teacher and the secretary of the Beginner department should make a list of the children who are to be promoted. They should include in the list each child's full name, address, telephone number, parents' names with their church affiliation, and any other information which they feel will help the Primary workers. They should give a copy of this list to the Primary superintendent at least a month before Promotion Day in order that she may form her classes and make plans for a happy and orderly reception of the children.

Sometimes it is helpful to include after each child's name some specific information about his abilities and interests. Occasionally it is to a child's advantage to include such a statement as: "Has been with us a year. Did not have experience in Nursery Class and has not been to kindergarten. Overprotected. Has not been allowed to use scissors at home but has learned to use his hands very well, considering his opportunities. Is developing some independence."

Because children often change completely in a new environment, teachers should be careful not to condemn in advance any child's behavior. If they think it is necessary to make any unfavorable comment, they should give it some such form as, "We have failed to help Lucy very much in recognizing property rights of others."

The secretary should order the certificates of promotion early and thus insure ample time to fill them out and have the pastor and general superintendent sign them without any last-minute confusion.

Prepare children for changes.—It is important also that the teachers carefully prepare the children for the changes which lie ahead. They will accept and look forward happily to Promotion Day and experiences that follow if the teachers will mention' the occasion frequently and make it clear to all that some will be promoted and others will stay to welcome a new group from the Cradle Roll department. The teachers should designate again and again the ones who are to be promoted, referring to them as "our graduates." At different times they may ask them to stand and sing songs of their own choosing, to show how tall they are, or to be counted. Such recognition adds to their feeling of the importance of the step they are soon to take and precludes disappointment for the children who are to remain in the department. It will help, too, if the teachers lead those in the younger group to make some simple parting gift for the graduates or to learn a song to sing to them.

Consider needs of new group.—In making plans the teachers should also consider the needs of the children who will remain in the department and those who will be promoted to it. Of course the work in the department will not be new to the Beginners who stay, but they may need help in making necessary adjustments after Promotion Day. To the Cradle Roll graduates everything will be strange and new unless the teachers take time and make opportunity to get acquainted with them in advance. A visit in the home of each child by the superintendent-teacher and the teacher to whose group he is to be assigned will be appreciated by the parents and will help in a great way to make the transition easy for the child. Sometimes the Cradle Roll and Beginner workers co-operate in giving a party for the Beginners-to-be and their mothers and find that the results more than justify their time and effort.

The superintendent-teacher should receive from the Cradle Roll superintendent a list of all the children who are to be promoted. This list, like the one she and the secretary prepare for the Primary superintendent, should contain in addition to accurate information about each child, a statement as to whether he has been a member of the Nursery Class.

Not all the children who receive certificates of promotion from the Cradle Roll department will be present on Promotion Sunday or the next Sunday. Doubtless there will be some who for various reasons may not come for several Sundays. This calls for very careful attention on the part of the teachers. If a child cannot come to Sunday school for a time, the teacher to whose group he is assigned may take the Sunday school to him by visiting in the home, taking him the *Beginner Bible Story* leaflets, and talking to him and his parents about the good times that await him in the department. It is most important in this and other ways to strengthen the tie which the Cradle Roll workers have established with the child and his home. If the tie is broken during this period of transition, the child and his parents may be lost to the church and its ministry.

Support general program plans.—When plans for Promotion Day are outlined by the officers and teachers of the school or by a special committee charged with this responsibility, Beginner teachers should accept them and cheerfully co-operate in promoting them. Such plans often provide for all the departments of the school to assemble and for the graduating group from each department to take some special part in the program. They often provide also for the certificates of promotion to be presented by the pastor or the general superintendent.

In large Sunday schools it may be more practical for each department to plan its own promotion service and conduct it in its own room. This plan necessitates a carefully made and consistently followed time schedule for the passing of groups from one department to another.

In either instance, the part the Beginners take in the program should be very simple and should require no drilling. The more natural the children can be, the better it will be for all concerned. Their contribution will be more meaningful to them if they can help to plan it and feel that they are sharing happy learnings with their friends and with one another.

PROMOTING CHRISTIAN HOME WEEK

Every child deserves a Christian home. It is his right.

The aim of Christian Home Week is to put special emphasis on the place and ministry of the Christian home in our whole educational program and to recognize Christ as the unseen guest at all times.

Workers should remember that every home needs God.

To insure best results, definite plans should be made well in advance.

The visiting of every home in the community, and of every church member, should be one of the main features of the week.

A letter may go out from the church office signed by the Beginner superintendent. It may be similar to the following:

DEAR————:

In her radio message to the British Empire on April 11, 1943, the Queen of England voiced a fundamental principle when she said: "If your homes can be truly Christian, there the influence of that spirit will assuredly spread like leaven through all the aspects of our common life—industrial, social, and political."

Our church is observing Christian Home Week, May ————. We are enclosing a program for the entire week. You will find a suggested schedule for each day. Follow the schedule and climax the week by attending the service on May——and sitting with your family. This is "Family-in-Church-Day." Our pastor is bringing a special message on the family. We are counting on you.

Cordially,

A SUGGESTED SCHEDULE
First Sunday

Morning.—Launch Christian Home Week in Sunday school. Distribute copies of the program for the week. The sermon may center around the home.

Afternoon.—Continue the visitation if necessary. A light lunch may be served at the church at noon for all visitors.

Evening.—Have special emphasis on the home in all assembly and union programs. The sermon may also be on the home.

Monday

Home Dedication Night.—Urge the church families to dedicate their homes to God.

Wednesday

Devote the prayer meeting to a promotion of the family altar in each home and daily private worship and individual Bible reading for each person.

Thursday and Friday

Suggest that each family observe one of these nights as Family-at-Home-Night. Ask every member of the family to remain at home for that evening. Utilize the occasion for family singing, games, a discussion of matters of interest to the family, the family altar—in short, for family fun, counsel and worship.

FAMILY-IN-CHURCH DAY

Christian Home Week may be climaxed with the services of the second Sunday. Emphasis should be placed on the family attending worship services and sitting together as a family group.

The Sunday before reminders in the shape of a church or home may be sent home by the Beginner. The reminder might read:

MAY 4-11

An Important Week
Why?
Christian Home Week

MAY 11

An Important Day
Why?
Family-in-Church Day

PROVIDING A VACATION BIBLE SCHOOL

Through the Vacation Bible school, the Sunday school extends its ministry to the children into the weekdays during public school vacation time. The schools are usually for two weeks, three hours a day, five days a week, and conducted in keeping with the promotional literature and textbooks provided by the Baptist Sunday School Board, and at the time most suitable for each school.

RECOGNIZING THE IMPORTANCE

The importance of the Vacation Bible School is obvious. It provides many extra hours for Bible teaching and training in Christlike living. It offers wholesome entertainment for the children at a time when those of school age are especially inclined to be restive. It gives opportunity for the pastor really to make friends with the children. His presence each morning and his position of leadership add dignity and importance to the school. A preacher who was inclined to be skeptical about the value of a school visited one in a neighboring church for several mornings and was impressed by the friendly greetings which pastor and children exchanged as the group assembled in front of the church. Later he saw the pastor take his place in the procession and lead the children into the church and down its quiet aisle. He saw him join with them in salutes to the United States flag, the Christian flag, and the Bible, and was persuaded that if the school provided only these contacts with the pastor it would be of inestimable value in all the church was trying to do for the children.

ACCEPTING THE CHALLENGE

The church should instruct the Sunday school to promote and conduct the Vacation Bible school as a unit of its work, doing so in keeping with the general plans provided in the Vacation Bible school literature. For the successful promotion of the school, however, much dependence must be placed on those who love little children and growing boys and girls, and understand how to work with them. The spirit with which they accept their work will largely characterize the spirit of the school.

Serve on the faculty.—The Vacation Bible school is organized by departments corresponding to the Beginner, Primary, Junior, and Intermediate departments of the Sunday school. As far as possible, the Beginner Sunday school teachers should also serve in the Beginner department of the Vacation school. The friendship that exists between them and the children is a great asset. They understand the children and know how best to deal with them. The children, in turn, are accustomed to their leadership, and this makes it possible for experiences in the Vacation school really to be an extension of the good times they have together on Sunday morning.

Contacts with the children day after day, the longer periods for work and play, and the variety of activities possible in connection with the weekday programs make the experience very valuable to the teachers as they seek to guide the children in their religious growth and development. During the ten days of the school with thirty hours of teaching opportunity, they can accomplish as much as during a much longer period in Sunday school with a whole week intervening between teaching periods.

If it is not possible for the Sunday school teachers to serve, they should cheerfully co-operate with the principal in securing the necessary number of dependable teachers.

Make plans in advance.—Usually the faculty begins preparation some weeks in advance of the opening of the school. This is necessary in order that all the workers may become thoroughly familiar with the purposes and plans, and so be prepared to co-operate wholeheartedly in promoting the work.

There are two textbooks for the Beginner department, to be used by the teachers in alternate years according to a schedule: Beginner Book A, *The Little Children's World,* and Beginner Book B, *Glad Days.* Pages 5-21 of both books are the same, being "A Manual for Beginner Workers in the Vacation Bible School." The manual sets forth in detail the plans for promoting and conducting the department, and the methods for using the program materials which make up the remainder of the textbook.

In making advance preparation the Beginner superintendent and her co-workers should carefully study the manual. They should also prepare handwork materials for the duration of the school, distribute responsibilities, and outline procedures.

Co-operate in daily schedule.—Beginner workers should co-operate with the principal and the workers of the other departments in adopting and abiding by the suggested daily schedule. This schedule provides for a definite opening and closing hour, and recess periods so planned that the activities of one group do not interfere with those of another. The schedule of activities for the various departments differ, but all departments usually take part in a general opening service. Following the close of each day's session, the faculty members meet in department groups to talk over the day's experiences and to make plans for the next day.

Conserve results of the school.—Often the Vacation Bible school enrols children who have not been reached for the Sunday school. The welcome they receive and the good times they have naturally awaken their interest in the other activities of the church. Thus, the children and their parents too become good prospects for the Sunday school, and are often easily enlisted.

New workers in the school should get excellent training for work in the Beginner department of the Sunday school. Enlisting them as regular workers, and using any methods and materials that have proved especially valuable, will also help to conserve the values of the school.

PARTICIPATING IN A TRAINING PROGRAM

Looking toward the highest degree of efficiency, every Sunday school should provide a regular program of training in which the workers of all departments participate. Of first importance in such a program are training schools where the workers gather in groups and study textbooks under the leadership of competent teachers. There are other means of growth, however, that also deserve special consideration.

STUDYING IN TRAINING SCHOOLS

Training schools should be held at least twice a year, preferably during the months of October and April. For use in this connection the Baptist Sunday School Board offers a Sunday School Training Course. The books in the course are arranged in six groups: Bible, Administration, Teaching, Doctrine and Evangelism, General Studies, and a specialization unit including books on administration and teaching as they pertain to the various departments of the school.

The weeks of special training may be held in co-operation with city-wide or association-wide plans, or the Sunday school may conduct its own training school. In either event, Beginner teachers and prospective teachers should avail themselves of the opportunity to increase their knowledge of the Bible and improve their skill in teaching it to little children. They should also seek in this way to gain a comprehensive view of the work of the Sunday school as a whole.

USING OTHER MEANS OF GROWTH

In promoting its program of training the Sunday school should also recognize and encourage the use of such other means of growth as needs may justify and local conditions may make possible.

Study the individual way.—In addition to studying in class groups, Beginner teachers may profit from the individual study of the books in the Sunday School Training Course. Such a plan makes it possible for them to finish the course and put their learnings into practice in a much shorter length of time. Full directions for doing the work in this way are given in the books.

The reading of additional desirable books is also a means of growth. The Baptist Book Stores in the various states carry an excellent line of books, new and old, about the Bible, books of personal devotions, books on child life, travel, mission, adventure, and others with special interest appeal for teachers of Beginners. Public and church libraries, if kept up to date, are also sources of help to those who wish to keep abreast with current thought in connection with their work.

Attend   conferences   and   conventions.—Attending Southwide and state Sunday school conferences and conventions is a particularly fine means of growth. The fellowship with large numbers of Christian workers, which such occasions afford, is in itself an enriching experience. Programs in connection with the meetings are always inspiring and helpful.

The general periods with their special speakers and discussions of matters pertaining to the whole school and conference periods devoted to department work combine to make the meetings of untold value to all who attend. Many Sunday schools recognize this fact and make it possible for representatives from the various departments to have experiences of this kind. Individuals also are quick to realize that attendance upon these meetings is a real investment in training.

The district Sunday school association is another avenue of growth. Offering as it does opportunities for the workers from all the churches in the association to meet regularly for consultation and the sharing of methods and materials, it gives promise of helpfulness which no Beginner teacher can afford to miss.

Observe others at work.—In many communities there is a really good nursery school or kindergarten which Beginner teachers can visit, and see informal yet orderly teaching under professional guidance.

Sunday school groups sometimes hold clinics for actual participation in working with children. One group, for example, met on a weekday for an expansion of the previous Sunday's session. This made it possible for the observers to see actual teaching and not merely an exhibition. After the session was over and the children had departed, those who had observed the teaching lingered to compare notes and evaluate the procedure.

It is of great value to the teachers to visit occasionally a department in another Sunday school. If they will remove their hats, allow themselves to be greeted as visitors, and then remain quietly in the background the presence of two or three will not upset a group of children. In experiences of this kind the observers frequently learn what should not be done as well as what should be done to achieve desired results.

Practice under guidance.—Yet another way in which teachers may co-operate to improve their teaching is to practice under guidance. One of the duties of the Beginner superintendent-teacher is to guide her teachers in their work. When she is impersonal and fair, her comments and suggestions should be appreciated and should help to keep the work of the department at the highest possible level. The teachers should, in turn, feel free to offer constructive and helpful comments of the superintendent-teacher's work. She should be just as ready to take a suggestion as to give one.

In addition to this open, frank, friendly atmosphere of helpfulness within the department, the teachers should take advantage of other opportunities to practice under guidance. Activities in which they may co-operate at summer assemblies, associational meetings, laboratory schools, and other occasions of similar nature are particularly helpful. It is also possible for teachers successfully to practice teaching under their own supervision. If they will make written plans for each Sunday and carefully keep records of their successes and failures, they can constantly improve the quality of their work.

Opportunities for Beginner teachers to co-operate with workers in other departments are not limited to the special occasions which have been discussed. There are many small ways in which the departments can work together and numerous friendly courtesies which they can exchange. All these experiences contribute to oneness of purpose and ability to achieve it.

The activities suggested in this and other chapters of the text presuppose the teachers' ever-increasing love for God and their close communion with him. They take for granted also the teachers' growing desire to serve little children and their willingness to give of themselves unstintingly in so doing.

Tomorrow is in the keeping of the children who are Beginners today and their fitness for the responsibilities of tomorrow depends in no small measure upon the spirit and faithfulness of Beginner teachers today. More than their best they cannot give and less than their best they dare not give.

QUESTIONS FOR REVIEW AND EXAMINATION

CHAPTER I

1. Children of what age are known as Beginners in a properly graded Sunday school?
2. In what respects are many of them really "beginners"?
3. Mention some ways in which the children differ.
4. How are mental differences particularly manifested?
5. What characteristics do the children have in common?
6. Why is it fortunate for teachers that the children have common interests and characteristics?
7. Upon what does each child's developing concept of God depend?
8. What is necessary to insure patterns of desirable conduct being carried over into the home?

CHAPTER II

1. On whom does responsibility for selecting and enlisting Beginner workers rest?
2. Why should great care be exercised in selecting the workers?
3. Mention four qualifications the workers should possess.
4. What qualifications combine to make a personality attractive to children?
5. How can workers be helped to feel the challenge of the task?
6. What organization is necessary to care for a department with an enrolment of twenty-five children?
7. Mention the duties of the office you hold or would like to hold.

CHAPTER III

1. Why is great importance attached to the room and equipment which a church provides for Beginners?

2. Mention three important considerations in connection with the location of the room.

3. What other matters should have careful attention in planning the room?

4. What three purposes should the furnishings of the room serve?

5. What special helps are offered for teachers and children in connection with the Beginner lesson course?

6. Mention other important helps which are offered for teachers and children.

7. What system of records is best suited for use in the department? How has it been adapted for Beginners?

8. Tell why play equipment should be provided and mention items that are particularly desirable.

CHAPTER IV

1. What should be given first place in the teaching materials used in a Beginner department?

2. Suggest ways in which teachers may lead the children to love and appreciate the Bible as "God's Book."

2. Mention other materials which may be used in guiding learning experiences.

4. What suggestion is offered for the use of materials?

5. What steps are necessary in connection with successfully engaging in an educative enterprise?

6. What requirements should be met by any trip planned for Beginners?

7. In what ways may the children be helped to rest and relax?

Chapter V

1. Why does music make a distinct contribution to Beginner department work?
2. For what purposes may music without words be used?
3. Mention the three suggestions offered in connection with choosing songs for Beginners.
4. Tell how songs should be used in the department.
5. What procedure should be followed in teaching a new song?
6. How may the teachers help the children to become familiar with the words of a new song?
7. For what purposes may songs be used in meeting program needs?
8. What is the loftiest purpose for which the children use songs?

Chapter VI

1. What is one of the richest gifts the children find in God's house?
2. Why is it important to relate worship to the children's everyday living?
3. What provisions should teachers make to insure worship on the part of the children?
4. Mention some ways in which God's presence may be made real to the children.
5. Mention two ways in which the teachers may contribute to quiet wonder.
6. In what ways may the children express worship in song?
7. What forms of prayer are especially suited to the children's use?
8. How may the children be guided in worshipful giving?

Chapter VII

1. What is the advantage of co-operation in making program plans?
2. Mention three suggestions offered in connection with lesson study.
3. What should influence the choice of possible activities?
4. What basic principles should be recognized in making program plans?
5. What elements are essential to every session and how should teachers plan for them?
6. To what end should teachers co-operate in using the plans?
7. Mention three suggestions offered in connection with using the plans.
8. Why is it helpful to evaluate a session? When should the evaluation take place?

Chapter VIII

1. Why do Beginner teachers find it profitable to meet for consultation and general planning with the general superintendent and the workers in other departments?
2. Under whose leadership should the weekly officers and teachers' meeting be held?
3. Who presides over the general assembly and what items of interest to Beginner teachers are discussed?
4. What suggestions are offered for making department periods interesting and helpful?
5. Mention briefly the suggested administrative or promotional objectives for the department.
6. Why should the Standard of Excellence be adopted as a guide to greater efficiency?
7. Under what conditions is it advisable to hold separate or special conferences for Beginner teachers?

8. What determines the blessings individual teachers receive from the weekly officers and teachers' meeting and the special Beginner conferences?

Chapter IX

1. Mention four special opportunities for co-operation between Beginner teachers and the workers in other departments.
2. What steps are necessary in making Promotion Day a happy occasion?
3. What is the purpose of Christian Home Week?
4. What suggestions are offered in connection with the program for the week?
5. Why is it important for the church to provide a Vacation Bible school?
6. What responsibilities do Beginner teachers have in connection with the Vacation Bible school?
7. What special benefits are in store for Beginner teachers who take part in training schools?
8. Mention other ways by which they may increase the efficiency of their work.